Practical Handbook
No 11

FIXTURES AND FITTINGS IN DATED HOUSES 1567-1763

Drawings by Linda Hall

Text by N W Alcock and Linda Hall

1994 (Reprinted 1999, 2002)
Council for British Archaeology

Published 1994 by the Council for British Archaeology
Bowes Morrell House, 111 Walmgate, York, YO1 9WA
Reprinted 1999, 2002

British Library Cataloguing in Publication Data
A catalogue card for this book is available from the British Library

ISBN 1 872414 52 4

Typeset by M C Bishop, Ryton, Tyne and Wear
Printed by Pennine Printing Services Limited,
Ripponden, West Yorkshire

Front cover: The Gables, Cromhall, Glos. 1669
Back cover: Cockshead Hinge from Moat House, Pucklechurch, Glos.
(Photos: L. Hall)

Contents

Introduction

The dating of historic buildings is one of the most important aspects of their study, and one of the most difficult. The knowledge needed to associate particular features with their likely date range can only be acquired through extensive field study of buildings for which dates are known, or at least are suggested. This handbook was initiated by the Historic Buildings Committee of the CBA to offer a partial answer to the problem. Like its companion volume, *Recording Timber-framed Buildings: an Illustrated Glossary* (N W Alcock, M W Barley, P W Dixon, R A Meeson; CBA Practical Handbook 5; 1989), it is intended primarily for those less rather than more experienced in the study of buildings. We hope that it will also be of value to those more expert, by providing evidence of the geographical and temporal spread of features that may only have been encountered in local contexts. It should also be of use as a record of typical (and some unusual) fittings for their own sake. In collecting this material, it has become apparent how rarely such items have been fully recorded. Such missed opportunities may never recur; these features are all too vulnerable to fashion, vandalism or profitable sale, even though the removal of fittings from listed buildings is illegal without listed building consent.

The handbook has been limited to buildings dated by inscription as the most specific indicators of the dates for features. However, readers should always remember the possibility of some particular feature not being of the same date as the rest of the building, or indeed of the inscription not relating to building work at all. The date range was originally intended to be 1550–1750, but no dated houses with useful detail could be found for the first decade of this period, while the final date has been extended to cover several interesting buildings of the 1750s. Earlier buildings of course also have interesting features, notably mouldings, windows and panelling, but their close dating is generally impossible. The criterion for accepting a building is specific: that it carries an inscribed date, and that the features recorded are believed to be of that date; buildings dated from documentary sources have been excluded because of the inevitable lack of certainty about the correlation of the existing building and the date. When there is an element of doubt about the date itself (eg with a reset or nearly illegible inscription), the date is marked with a query, as are the captions of any drawings where the association of the feature and the date is not entirely certain; these can be distinguished from the gazetteer at the end of the handbook where uncertain dates are again marked with a query. The possibility of fittings such as dressers, panelling or hinges being inserted as well as removed should also be remembered.

The handbook covers all sorts of fixtures, fittings and decorative details, including beam and mullion mouldings (as well as mouldings on fittings), but plasterwork and painted decoration are excluded, as are structural details such as roof trusses, framing and bracing and joints; these show much more regional differentiation than do purely decorative features. Coverage is broadly restricted to fittings of wood, by far the most frequently used material for decoration, and of iron; some occurrences in stone of mouldings also used for wood have been included. It might be possible in the future to bring together a companion collection of stone details, such as doorcases, fireplaces, window labels, mullions, string courses, finials, kneelers and chimney caps, though it is worth noting that timber detailing is much more widely distributed geographically than decorative stonework. The buildings from which material is drawn are principally vernacular in scale with some of 'gentry' status, but excluding 'great houses'.

The arrangement of drawings is thematic, moving from stairs to doors and windows and their associated fittings and details, and then to fixed furniture such as cupboards and dressers; panelling, friezes and overmantels are associated with these fittings because of the similarity in their decorative motifs, and finally general decoration such as mouldings and stops is covered. When no sub-types are identified, the sections of each drawing are generally arranged in date order. The number of illustrations of different items does not reflect their importance, nor their frequency of survival, as much as the scope they offer for decorative variation and embellishment. For common features, one typical example is shown together with an indication of the date range. It should be noted that many of the drawings have been made from photographs, and the dimensions may not be precise. The nomenclature follows that of *Recording Timber-framed Buildings*, with any additional terms given in the figure captions.

The gazetteer lists the 400 buildings used, and provides an index to the drawings and to the additional occurrences listed in the captions. Historic counties have been used throughout because much of the material used (especially that from Wales) was arranged on that basis. The examples (map opposite) are very widely distributed in England and Wales, being drawn from 38 counties. Scotland is not included because of the almost entirely different date range for its buildings.

The distribution is far from even. This undoubtedly reflects the irregular distribution of dated buildings themselves, but equally important is the distribution of fieldwork and the availability of detailed information on

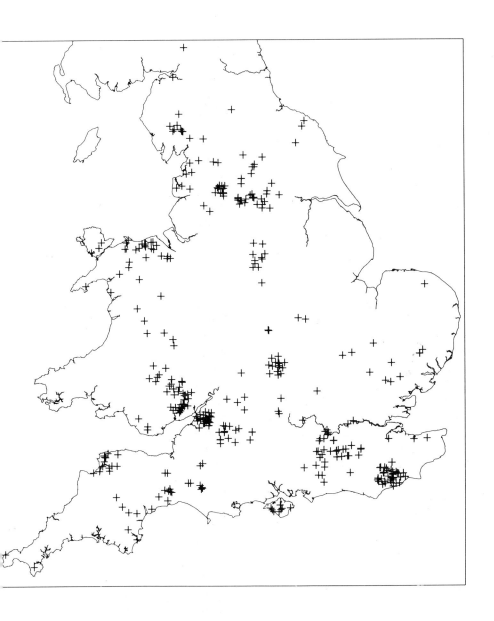

Distribution map of dated houses (Coastline: Copyright Bartholemew Database)

fittings. Some features appear to have a regional distribution which in reality reflects only the limitations of the evidence; for example, acorn stair finials are found in the Lake District as well as southern England, but none have been noted in dated houses.

Sources

Most of the buildings described are unpublished and information has been provided by individuals, to all of whom we are extremely grateful. Some information has been obtained from the National Buildings Record, but this has not been searched comprehensively. The principal contributors have been: A Armstrong; M Birdsall; A Brodie; H Brooksby; V Chesher; S Denyer; R Gibson; J Harding (and the Surrey Domestic Buildings Recording Group); B Hutton; S Jones; S Kholucy (and SPAB students); M McClintock; D and B Martin; R Mather; J Moir; C North; J Penoyre; M Roberts; P Slocombe (and the Wiltshire Buildings Record); P Thornborow; T Tolhurst; R Tyler; J Wade.

Bibliography

The following works provide the most extensive published compilations of dated buildings; for the present volume they have been supplemented by reference to the corresponding primary fieldwork records; these are held by L. Hall (Gloucestershire and Avon), D and B Martin (Sussex), the National Museum of Wales, Cardiff (Monmouthshire) and the Royal Commission on the Ancient and Historical Monuments of Wales, Aberystwyth (Wales).

Brinton, Marion, *Farmhouses and Cottages of the Isle of Wight*, Isle of Wight County Council, 1987

Fox, Sir Cyril and Raglan, Lord, *Monmouthshire Houses*, National Museum of Wales: Cardiff, 1951–1954.

Hall, Linda J, *The Rural Houses of North Avon and South Gloucestershire: 1400–1720*, City of Bristol Museum & Art Gallery: Bristol, 1983.

Martin, David and Barbara, A selection of dated houses in Eastern Sussex: 1400–1750, *Historic buildings in Eastern Sussex*, vol 4, 1987, 1–140.

Smith, Peter, *Houses of the Welsh Countryside*, HMSO: London, 2nd ed 1988.

Wood-Jones, R B, *Traditional Domestic Architecture in the Banbury Region*, Manchester University Press, 1963 [RWJ in Gazetteer]

For chamfer stops, see especially Jones, S R and Smith, J T, Chamfer-stops: a provisional mode of reference, *Vernacular Architecture*, 2, 12–15 (1971). [SRJ in Gazetteer]

1 – Turned Balusters

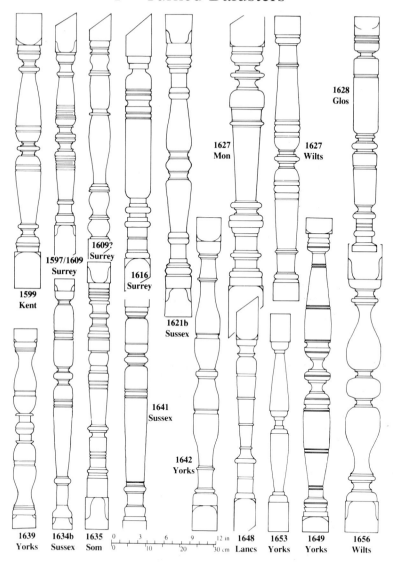

1628
Glos

1627
Mon

1627
Wilts

1609?
Surrey

1597/1609
Surrey

1599
Kent

1616
Surrey

1621b
Sussex

1641
Sussex

1642
Yorks

1639
Yorks

1634b
Sussex

1635
Som

1648
Lancs

1653
Yorks

1649
Yorks

1656
Wilts

0   3   6   9   12 in
0   10   20   30 cm

1

2 – Turned Balusters

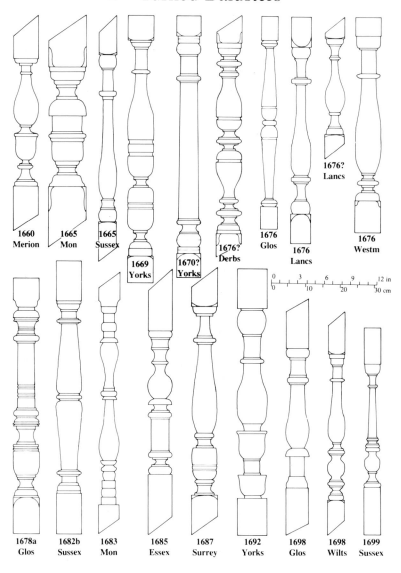

1676?
Lancs

1660 Merion	1665 Mon	1665 Sussex				1676 Glos		1676 Westm

1669 Yorks

1670? Yorks

1676? Derbs

1676 Lancs

0		3		6		9		12 in
0		10			20			30 cm

1678a Glos	1682b Sussex	1683 Mon	1685 Essex	1687 Surrey	1692 Yorks	1698 Glos	1698 Wilts	1699 Sussex

3 – Turned Balusters

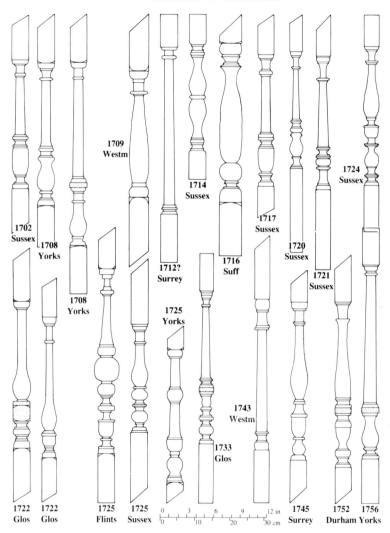

1709
Westm

1714
Sussex

1702
Sussex

1708
Yorks

1724
Sussex

1717
Sussex

1720
Sussex

1712?
Surrey

1716
Suff

1721
Sussex

1708
Yorks

1725
Yorks

1743
Westm

1733
Glos

| 1722 | 1722 | 1725 | 1725 | 0   3   6   9   12 in | 1745 | 1752 | 1756 |
| Glos | Glos | Flints | Sussex | 0 10 20 30 cm | Surrey | Durham | Yorks |

Turned balusters with square unturned blocks (stippled). Other examples: 1731 Sussex (p 4); 1738 Yorks; 1744 Sussex (p 4); 1748 Yorks. 1676 Glos: the balusters are of a ventilation grille (pp 2 and 19).

4 – Twisted Balusters

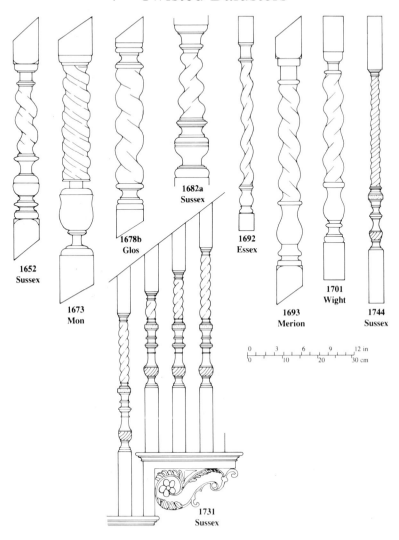

1652
Sussex

1673
Mon

1678b
Glos

1682a
Sussex

1692
Essex

1693
Merion

1701
Wight

1744
Sussex

1731
Sussex

1652 Sussex: This early date is carved on the newel post.
Additional examples: 1691 Wilts; 1693 Brecon; 1707 Norf; 1710 Cambs; 1718
London

5 – Carved Balusters

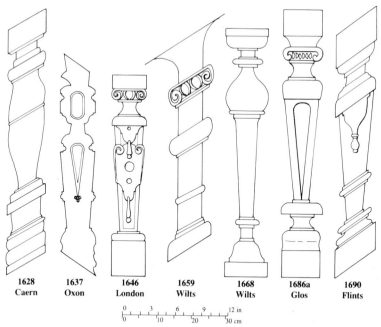

| 1628 | 1637 | 1646 | 1659 | 1668 | 1686a | 1690 |
| Caern | Oxon | London | Wilts | Wilts | Glos | Flints |

Fretwork Balustrade

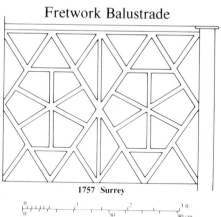

1757 Surrey

Carved balusters are rectangular in section, shaped on all four sides, while splat (flat) balusters are made from a plank, shaped to imitate turning and often pierced.

6 – Splat Balusters

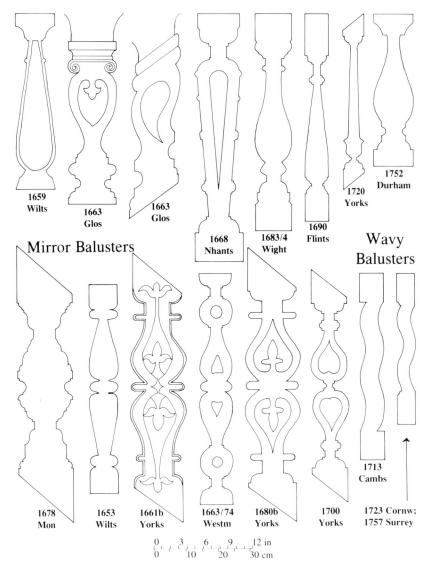

1659 Wilts

1663 Glos

1663 Glos

1668 Nhants

1683/4 Wight

1690 Flints

1720 Yorks

1752 Durham

Mirror Balusters

Wavy Balusters

1678 Mon

1653 Wilts

1661b Yorks

1663/74 Westm

1680b Yorks

1700 Yorks

1713 Cambs

1723 Cornw; 1757 Surrey

0   3   6   9   12 in
0   10   20   30 cm

1659 Wilts: balusters of a dog-gate; stair balusters carved (p 5)
1752 Durham: dresser support (p 45); 1690 Flints: dog-gate

6

7 – Strings

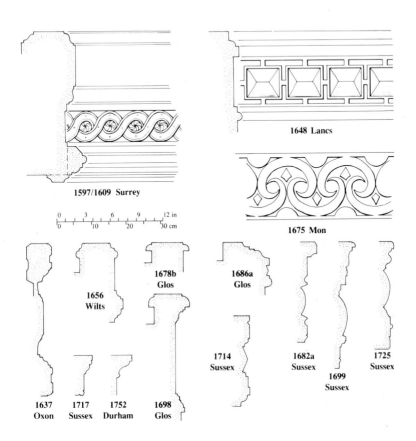

1648 Lancs

1597/1609 Surrey

1675 Mon

1678b
Glos

1686a
Glos

1656
Wilts

1714
Sussex

1682a
Sussex

1725
Sussex

1699
Sussex

1637
Oxon

1717
Sussex

1752
Durham

1698
Glos

8 – Handrails

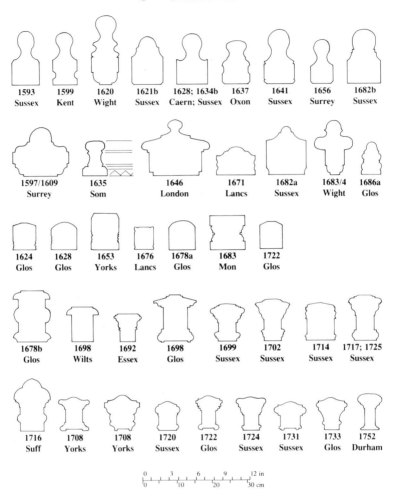

| 1593 Sussex | 1599 Kent | 1620 Wight | 1621b Sussex | 1628; 1634b Caern; Sussex | 1637 Oxon | 1641 Sussex | 1656 Surrey | 1682b Sussex |

| 1597/1609 Surrey | 1635 Som | 1646 London | 1671 Lancs | 1682a Sussex | 1683/4 Wight | 1686a Glos |

| 1624 Glos | 1628 Glos | 1653 Yorks | 1676 Lancs | 1678a Glos | 1683 Mon | 1722 Glos |

| 1678b Glos | 1698 Wilts | 1692 Essex | 1698 Glos | 1699 Sussex | 1702 Sussex | 1714 Sussex | 1717; 1725 Sussex |

| 1716 Suff | 1708 Yorks | 1708 Yorks | 1720 Sussex | 1722 Glos | 1724 Sussex | 1731 Sussex | 1733 Glos | 1752 Durham |

Bottom two rows: composite handrails, with mouldings applied to a rectangular block.

8

9 – Open String Brackets and Ramped Handrail

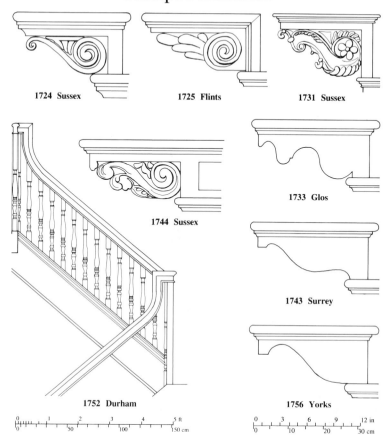

1724 Sussex

1725 Flints

1731 Sussex

1733 Glos

1744 Sussex

1743 Surrey

1752 Durham

1756 Yorks

Other ramped handrails: 1708 Yorks; 1716 Yorks; 1720 Sussex; 1721 Sussex; 1724 Sussex; 1725 Flints; 1731 Devon; 1731 Sussex; 1733 Glos; 1743 Surrey; 1744 Sussex; 1756 Yorks
Other open string stairs: 1707 Norf; 1710 Cambs; 1716 Yorks; 1720 Sussex; 1721 Sussex; 1743 Westm

9

10 – Finials

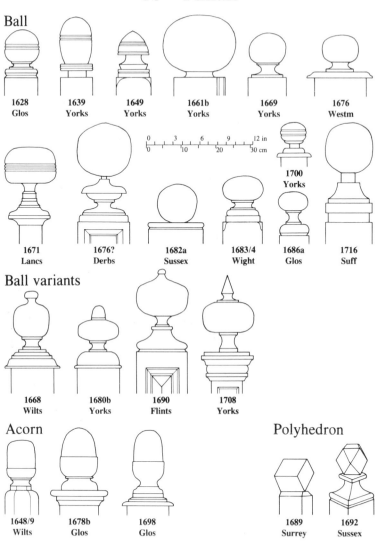

Ball

| 1628 Glos | 1639 Yorks | 1649 Yorks | 1661b Yorks | 1669 Yorks | 1676 Westm |

| 1671 Lancs | 1676? Derbs | 1682a Sussex | 1683/4 Wight | 1686a Glos | 1716 Suff |

1700 Yorks

Ball variants

| 1668 Wilts | 1680b Yorks | 1690 Flints | 1708 Yorks |

Acorn

| 1648/9 Wilts | 1678b Glos | 1698 Glos |

Polyhedron

| 1689 Surrey | 1692 Sussex |

Other acorn finials: 1665 Devon

10

11 – Finials

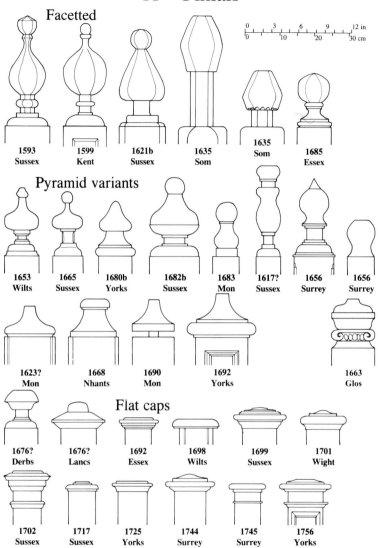

Facetted

| 1593 Sussex | 1599 Kent | 1621b Sussex | 1635 Som | 1635 Som | 1685 Essex |

Pyramid variants

| 1653 Wilts | 1665 Sussex | 1680b Yorks | 1682b Sussex | 1683 Mon | 1617? Sussex | 1656 Surrey | 1656 Surrey |

| 1623? Mon | 1668 Nhants | 1690 Mon | 1692 Yorks | 1663 Glos |

Flat caps

| 1676? Derbs | 1676? Lancs | 1692 Essex | 1698 Wilts | 1699 Sussex | 1701 Wight |

| 1702 Sussex | 1717 Sussex | 1725 Yorks | 1744 Surrey | 1745 Surrey | 1756 Yorks |

0   3   6   9   12 in
0   10   20   30 cm

11

12 – Pendants

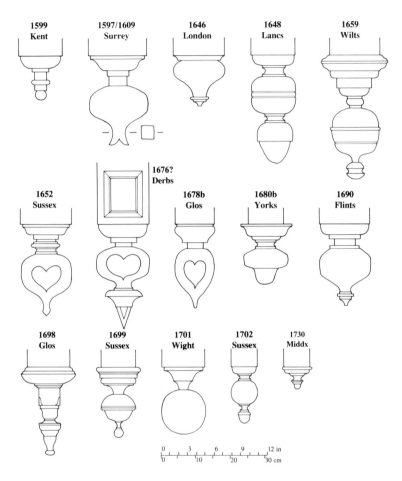

Newel posts with sunk panels: *1660 Merion; 1673 Mon; 1676 Derbs; 1690 Flints;*
1692 Yorks; 1708 Yorks; 1756 Yorks

13 – Newel Posts

1616 Surrey

1634b Sussex

1678 Mon

1648 Lancs

1637 Oxon

1628 Caern

1673 Mon

1597/1609 Surrey

1641 Sussex

1627 Mon

1652 Sussex

1646 London

1641 Sussex similar to 1634b Sussex. Stair forms (for examples see p 58): Open well, 1597–1744 (13a). Dog-leg, 1593–1756 (13b). Closed well, 1582 Brecon; 1664b Glos (13c)

14 – Plank and Batten Doors

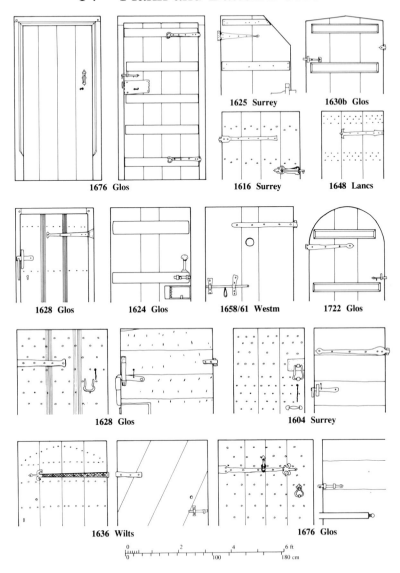

1676 Glos

1625 Surrey

1630b Glos

1616 Surrey

1648 Lancs

1628 Glos

1624 Glos

1658/61 Westm

1722 Glos

1628 Glos

1604 Surrey

1636 Wilts

1676 Glos

Plank and batten doors recorded at all dates
Other double-thickness doors: 1591 Devon; 1624 Glos; 1634b Sussex; 1669 Sussex;
1674 Glos; 1743 Westm

15 – Plank and Batten Doors with Applied Fillets

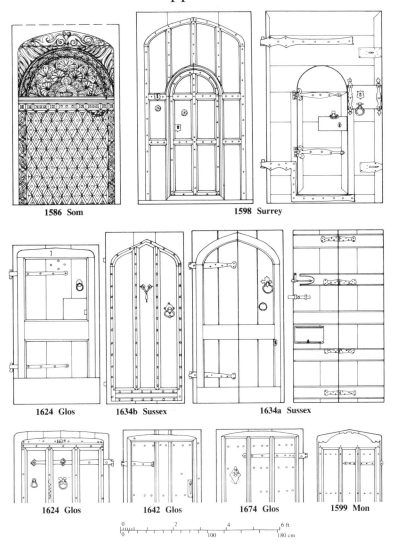

1586 Som

1598 Surrey

1624 Glos

1634b Sussex

1634a Sussex

1624 Glos

1642 Glos

1674 Glos

1599 Mon

0   2   4   6 ft
0   100   180 cm

16 – Decorative Doors with Applied Fillets

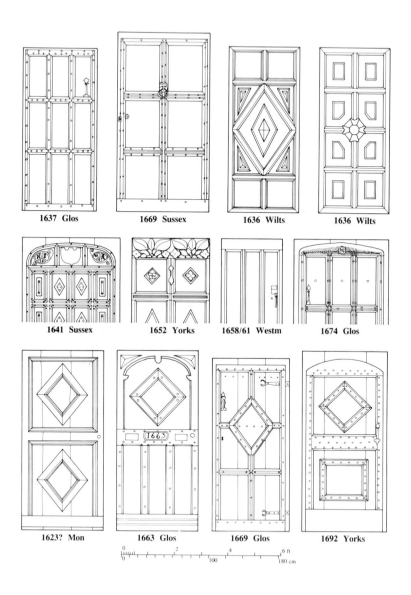

1637 Glos   1669 Sussex   1636 Wilts   1636 Wilts

1641 Sussex   1652 Yorks   1658/61 Westm   1674 Glos

1623? Mon   1663 Glos   1669 Glos   1692 Yorks

16

17 – Panelled Doors with True and False Panelling

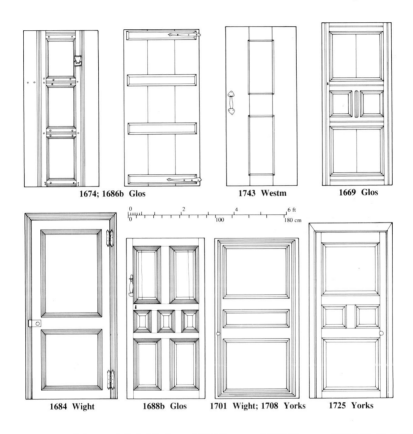

1674; 1686b Glos   1743 Westm   1669 Glos

1684 Wight   1688b Glos   1701 Wight; 1708 Yorks   1725 Yorks

Other two-panel doors: 1693 Merion; 1698 Lancs; 1699 Sussex; 1716 Suff; 1720 Sussex; 1743 Surrey; 1745 Suff; 1745 Surrey; 1757 Surrey

18 – Panelled Doors with True Panelling

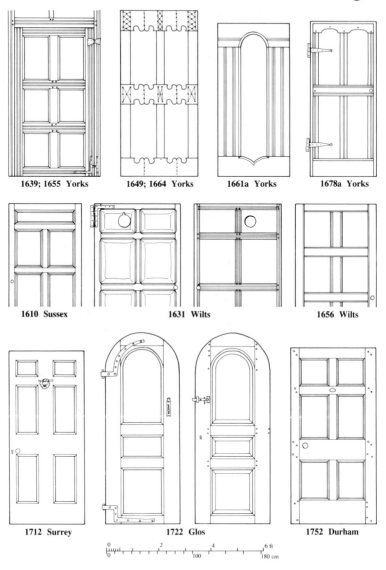

| 1639; 1655 Yorks | 1649; 1664 Yorks | 1661a Yorks | 1678a Yorks |

| 1610 Sussex | 1631 Wilts | 1656 Wilts |

| 1712 Surrey | 1722 Glos | 1752 Durham |

0 2 4 6 ft
0 100 180 cm

18

19 – Ventilated Doors and Grilles

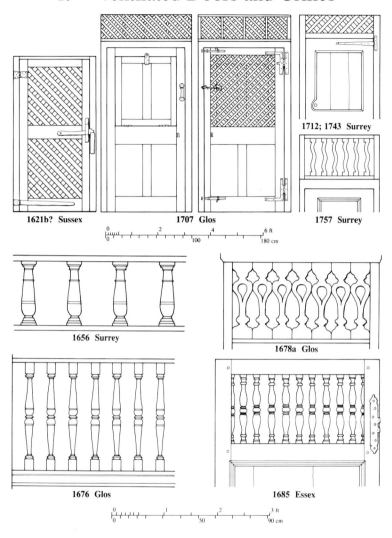

1621b? Sussex

1707 Glos

1712; 1743 Surrey

1757 Surrey

1656 Surrey

1678a Glos

1676 Glos

1685 Essex

Lattice grille: 1727 Wight

19

20 – Doorheads

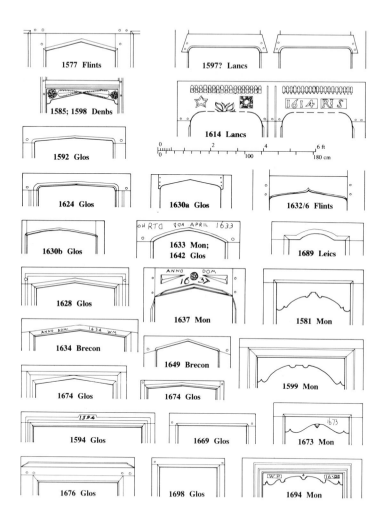

1577 Flints

1597? Lancs

1585; 1598 Denbs

1614 Lancs

1592 Glos

1624 Glos

1630a Glos

1632/6 Flints

1630b Glos

1633 Mon;
1642 Glos

1689 Leics

1628 Glos

1637 Mon

1581 Mon

1634 Brecon

1649 Brecon

1599 Mon

1674 Glos

1674 Glos

1594 Glos

1669 Glos

1673 Mon

1676 Glos

1698 Glos

1694 Mon

21 – Strap Hinges

Plain

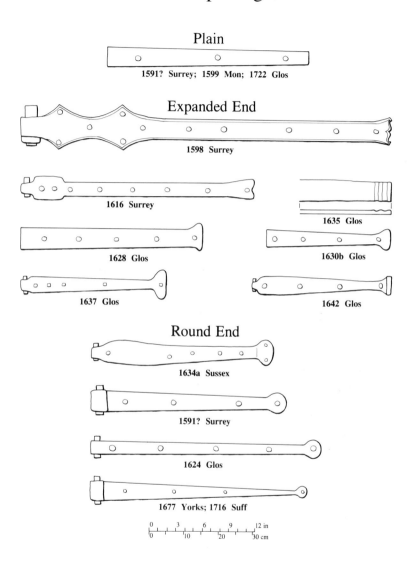

1591? Surrey; 1599 Mon; 1722 Glos

Expanded End

1598 Surrey

1616 Surrey

1635 Glos

1628 Glos

1630b Glos

1637 Glos

1642 Glos

Round End

1634a Sussex

1591? Surrey

1624 Glos

1677 Yorks; 1716 Suff

22 – Strap Hinges

Lozenge

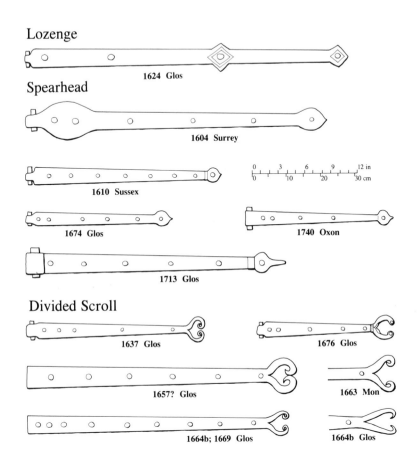

1624 Glos

Spearhead

1604 Surrey

1610 Sussex

1674 Glos

1740 Oxon

1713 Glos

Divided Scroll

1637 Glos

1676 Glos

1657? Glos

1663 Mon

1664b; 1669 Glos

1664b Glos

*Other spearhead hinges: 1583 Denbs; 1591 Surrey; 1599 Mon; 1627 Mon; 1629
Westm; 1658/61 Westm; 1664a Glos; 1666 Surrey; 1669 Sussex; 1677 Yorks;
1698 Glos; 1698 Lancs; 1722 Glos; 1733 Glos; 1743 Westm
Lozenge: 1629 Westm*

23 – Strap Hinges

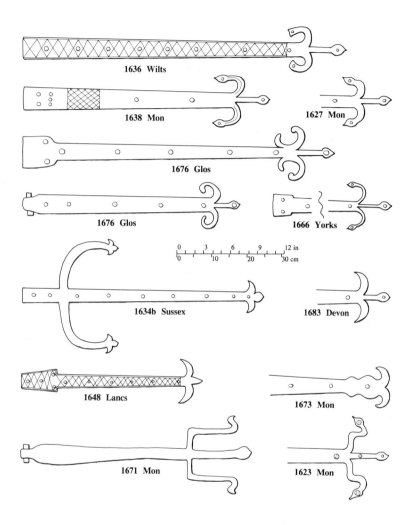

1636 Wilts

1638 Mon

1627 Mon

1676 Glos

1676 Glos

1666 Yorks

1634b Sussex

1683 Devon

1648 Lancs

1673 Mon

1671 Mon

1623 Mon

24 – Strap Hinges with Base-plates

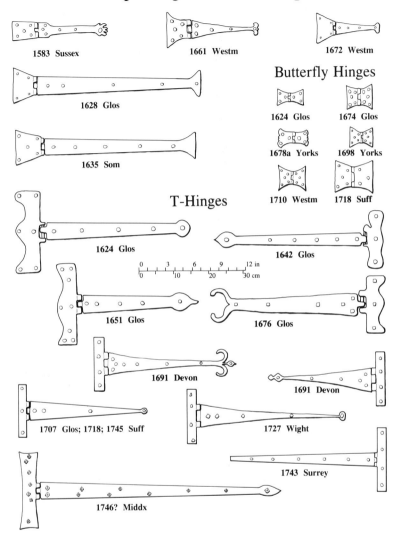

1583 Sussex

1661 Westm

1672 Westm

1628 Glos

Butterfly Hinges

1624 Glos

1674 Glos

1678a Yorks

1698 Yorks

1710 Westm

1718 Suff

1635 Som

T-Hinges

1624 Glos

1642 Glos

1651 Glos

1676 Glos

1691 Devon

1691 Devon

1707 Glos; 1718; 1745 Suff

1727 Wight

1743 Surrey

1746? Middx

Other butterfly hinges: 1625? Yorks; 1627b Devon; 1639 Yorks; 1658/61 Westm; 1669 Glos; 1688a Glos; 1725 Sussex; 1727 Wight; 1730 Middx

25 – Hinges

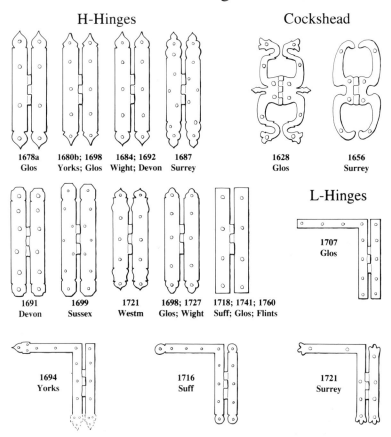

H-Hinges

1678a	1680b; 1698	1684; 1692	1687
Glos	Yorks; Glos	Wight; Devon	Surrey

1691	1699	1721	1698; 1727	1718; 1741; 1760
Devon	Sussex	Westm	Glos; Wight	Suff; Glos; Flints

Cockshead

1628	1656
Glos	Surrey

L-Hinges

1707
Glos

1694	1716	1721
Yorks	Suff	Surrey

Other examples: Cockshead hinges: 1633 Derbs; 1639 Yorks.
Plain H-hinges: 1725 Sussex; 1743 Westm; 1752 Durham.
Plain L-hinges: 1730 Surrey; 1731 Sussex; 1743 Surrey; 1745 Surrey
H-hinges and L-hinges may be 4 to 10 ins long (not drawn to scale).

26 – Door-handles

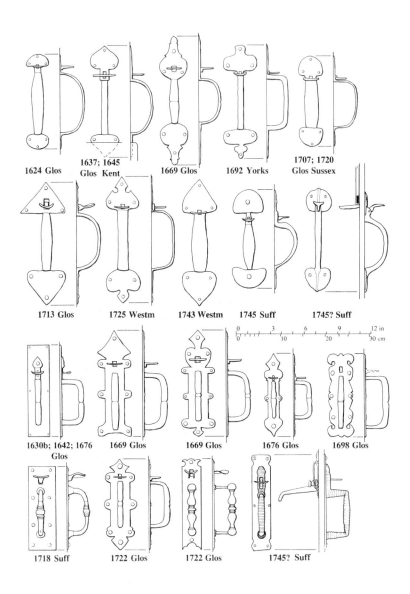

1624 Glos   1637; 1645 Glos Kent   1669 Glos   1692 Yorks   1707; 1720 Glos Sussex

1713 Glos   1725 Westm   1743 Westm   1745 Suff   1745? Suff

1630b; 1642; 1676 Glos   1669 Glos   1669 Glos   1676 Glos   1698 Glos

1718 Suff   1722 Glos   1722 Glos   1745? Suff

27 – Drop handles and Door-knockers

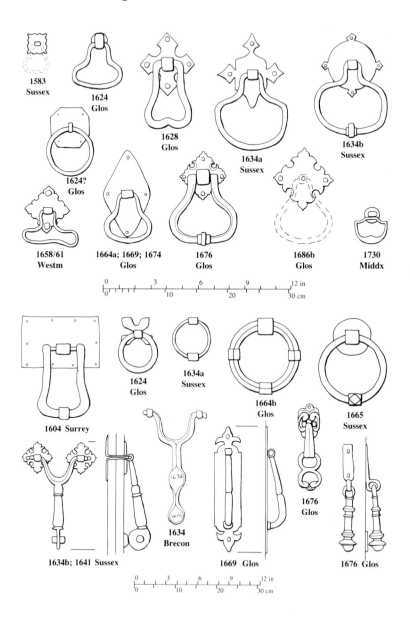

1583
Sussex

1624
Glos

1628
Glos

1634b
Sussex

1634a
Sussex

1624?
Glos

1658/61
Westm

1664a; 1669; 1674
Glos

1676
Glos

1686b
Glos

1730
Middx

0   3   6   9   12 in
0   10   20   30 cm

1604 Surrey

1624
Glos

1634a
Sussex

1664b
Glos

1665
Sussex

1634b; 1641 Sussex

1634
Brecon

1669 Glos

1676
Glos

1676 Glos

0   3   6   9   12 in
0   10   20   30 cm

27

28 – Latches

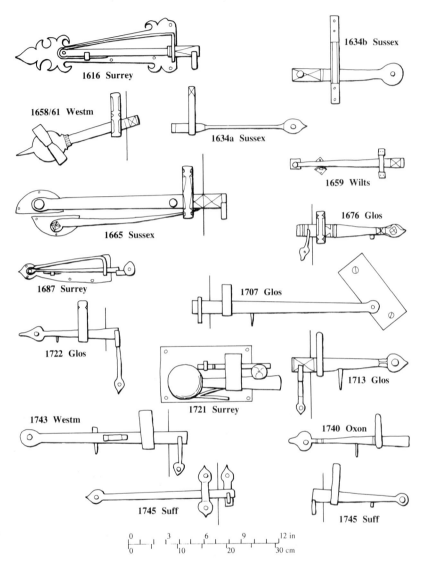

1616 Surrey

1634b Sussex

1658/61 Westm

1634a Sussex

1659 Wilts

1665 Sussex

1676 Glos

1687 Surrey

1707 Glos

1722 Glos

1713 Glos

1721 Surrey

1743 Westm

1740 Oxon

1745 Suff

1745 Suff

Drop handle fastened directly to latch: 1658/61 Westm; operating a pivot: 1659 Wilts; raising a bar: 1665 Sussex; operating a spring latch: 1616 Surrey; 1687 Surrey

29 – Wooden Latches and Handles

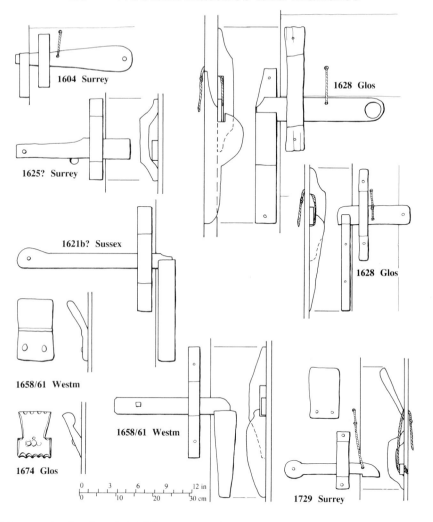

1604 Surrey

1628 Glos

1625? Surrey

1621b? Sussex

1628 Glos

1658/61 Westm

1658/61 Westm

1674 Glos

1729 Surrey

Other wooden latches: 1629 Westm; 1656 Surrey; 1666 Surrey; 1697 Westm; 1698 Lancs; 1743 Westm

30 – Bolts

Rectangular Section

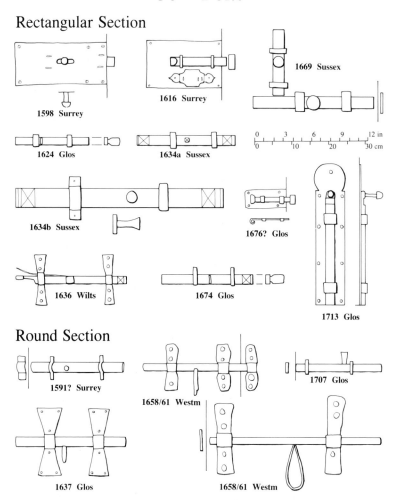

1598 Surrey

1616 Surrey

1669 Sussex

1624 Glos

1634a Sussex

1634b Sussex

1676? Glos

1636 Wilts

1674 Glos

1713 Glos

Round Section

1591? Surrey

1658/61 Westm

1707 Glos

1637 Glos

1658/61 Westm

1598 Surrey: bolt set into door

30

31 – Window Handles and Stays

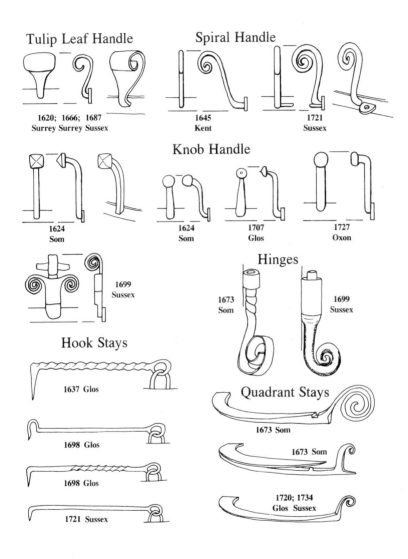

Tulip Leaf Handle

1620; 1666; 1687
Surrey Surrey Sussex

Spiral Handle

1645
Kent

1721
Sussex

Knob Handle

1624
Som

1624
Som

1707
Glos

1727
Oxon

1699
Sussex

Hinges

1673
Som

1699
Sussex

Hook Stays

1637 Glos

1698 Glos

1698 Glos

1721 Sussex

Quadrant Stays

1673 Som

1673 Som

1720; 1734
Glos Sussex

32 – Window Catches

Turnbuckles

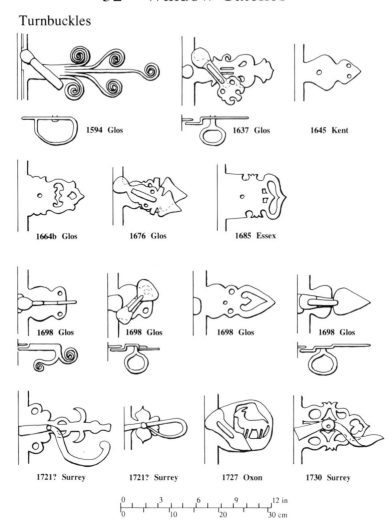

1594 Glos

1637 Glos

1645 Kent

1664b Glos

1676 Glos

1685 Essex

1698 Glos

1698 Glos

1698 Glos

1698 Glos

1721? Surrey

1721? Surrey

1727 Oxon

1730 Surrey

Some catches have lost their revolving turnbuckles.

33 – Window Catches

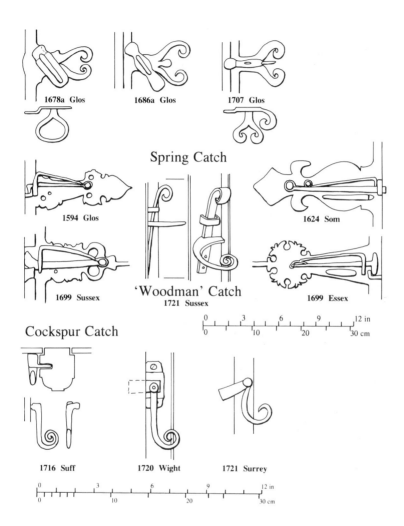

1678a Glos

1686a Glos

1707 Glos

Spring Catch

1594 Glos

1624 Som

1699 Sussex

'Woodman' Catch
1721 Sussex

1699 Essex

Cockspur Catch

1716 Suff

1720 Wight

1721 Surrey

34 – Lock-plates; Latch Fasteners

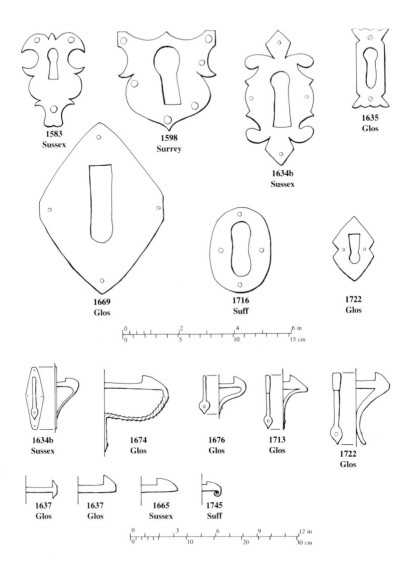

1583
Sussex

1598
Surrey

1635
Glos

1634b
Sussex

1669
Glos

1716
Suff

1722
Glos

0 2 4 6 in
0 5 10 15 cm

1634b
Sussex

1674
Glos

1676
Glos

1713
Glos

1722
Glos

1637
Glos

1637
Glos

1665
Sussex

1745
Suff

0 3 6 9 12 in
0 10 20 30 cm

34

35 – Stops – Doorframes

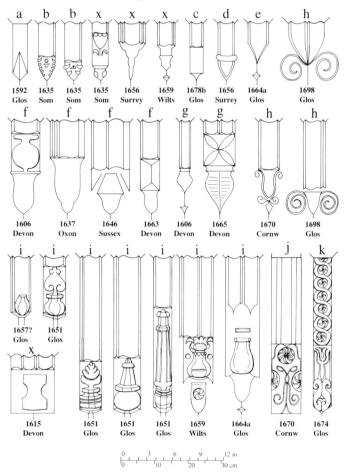

a	b	b	x	x	x	c	d	e	h
1592 Glos	1635 Som	1635 Som	1635 Som	1656 Surrey	1659 Wilts	1678b Glos	1656 Surrey	1664a Glos	1698 Glos

f	f	f	f	g	g	h	h
1606 Devon	1637 Oxon	1646 Sussex	1663 Devon	1606 Devon	1665 Devon	1670 Cornw	1698 Glos

i	i	i	i	i	i	i	j	k
1657? Glos	1651 Glos							

x

| 1615 Devon | 1651 Glos | 1651 Glos | 1651 Glos | 1659 Wilts | 1664a Glos | 1670 Cornw | 1674 Glos |

| 0 | 3 | 6 | 9 | 12 in |
| 0 | 10 | 20 | 30 cm |

a) Broach or pyramid b) Enriched runout c) Roll and flat d) Converging stop with bar e) Converging stop with nick f) Scroll variants g) Bar, leaf and nick h) Incised scrolls i) Pumpkin (vase, onion) and variants (1576–1678) j) Incised k) Tulip x) Unclassified

Pumpkin stops: rare on beams. On doorframes: 1576 Sussex; 1600 Glam; 1604 Surrey; 1609a Surrey; 1616 Surrey; 1621 Devon; 1622a Surrey; 1623 Surrey; 1625 Surrey. On stone fireplaces: 1594 Glos; 1612 Sussex; 1621b Sussex; 1631 Wilts; 1634b Sussex; 1648/9 Wilts; 1664b Glos; 1668 Wilts; 1669 Sussex; 1678b Glos

35

36 – Stops – Beams and doorframes

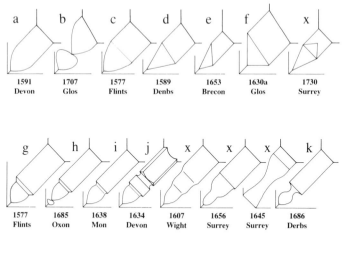

a	b	c	d	e	f	x
1591	1707	1577	1589	1653	1630a	1730
Devon	Glos	Flints	Denbs	Brecon	Glos	Surrey

g	h	i	j	x	x	x	k
1577	1685	1638	1634	1607	1656	1645	1686
Flints	Oxon	Mon	Devon	Wight	Surrey	Surrey	Derbs

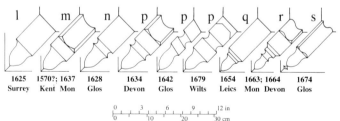

l	m	n	p	p	p	q	r	s
1625	1570?; 1637	1628	1634	1642	1679	1654	1663; 1664	1674
Surrey	Kent Mon	Glos	Devon	Glos	Wilts	Leics	Mon Devon	Glos

```
0        3        6        9      12 in
0          10         20        30 cm
```

*a) Runout (1607–1707) b) Runout and notch c) Angled runout (1619–1667)
d) Straight cut (45°) (1601; 1619) e) Diagonal cut f) Straight cut (90°) g) Step
(step and runout; step and hollow; Wern-hir; fillet and tongue) (1571–1739)
h) Step and nick i) Rounded step (1651; 1656) j) Rounded step, flat and bar
k) Leaf l) Scroll (cyma, lamb's tongue) (1591–1763) m) Scroll and flat
(1624–1688) n) Scroll and bar (1638–1683) p) Scroll, bar and flat (also scroll,
flat and bar) q) Scroll and step (1668; 1698) r) Scroll, bar, step and flat (1664)
s) Scroll and nick (1674–1698) x) Unclassified
For examples see page 58.*

36

37 – Stops – Beams and doorframes

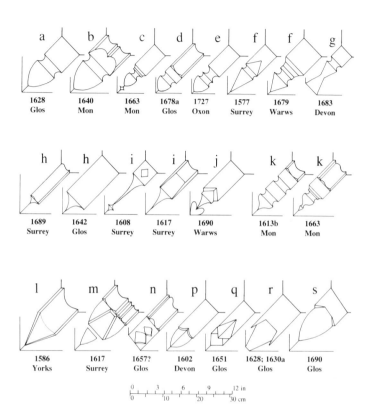

a	b	c	d	e	f	f	g
1628 Glos	1640 Mon	1663 Mon	1678a Glos	1727 Oxon	1577 Surrey	1679 Warws	1683 Devon

h	h	i	i	j	k	k
1689 Surrey	1642 Glos	1608 Surrey	1617 Surrey	1690 Warws	1613b Mon	1663 Mon

l	m	n	p	q	r	s
1586 Yorks	1617 Surrey	1657? Glos	1602 Devon	1651 Glos	1628; 1630a Glos	1690 Glos

a) Bar (bar and runout) (1583–1689); Bar and nick (not illustrated; 1664)
b) Enriched bar c) Step, bar and nick d) Bar and flat (1609–1678) e) Double bar
f) Straight cut and bar g) Bar and hourglass h) Roll (1671/3); Roll and flat (not
illustrated; 1678) i) Elongated roll and nick j) Enriched roll and notch k) Bar
variants l) Converging (sharply angled or smoothly curved; 1616–1698);
Converging with step (1582) and Converging with nick (1594) (not illustrated)
m) Interrupted runout with raised trapezoidal block n) Lozenge on flat p) Keeled
(1633) q) Pyramid (broach) (1592; 1615) r) Geometric (1630) s) Shouldered step
(1646; 1674) x) Unclassified
For examples see page 59.

38 – Mullions

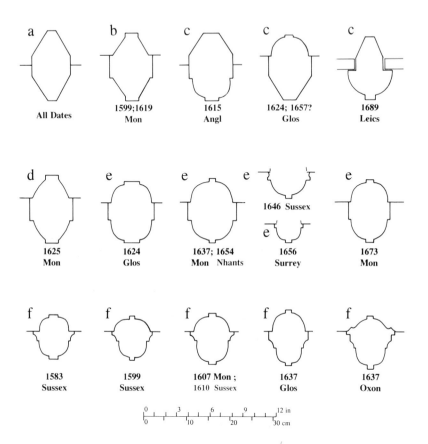

a	b	c	c	c
All Dates	1599;1619 Mon	1615 Angl	1624; 1657? Glos	1689 Leics

d	e	e	e	e
			1646 Sussex	
			e	
1625 Mon	1624 Glos	1637; 1654 Mon Nhants	1656 Surrey	1673 Mon

f	f	f	f	f
1583 Sussex	1599 Sussex	1607 Mon ; 1610 Sussex	1637 Glos	1637 Oxon

Includes both wooden and stone mullions; exterior faces towards top
a) Chamfered (flat splay): All dates (eg 1593–1750 in Banbury Region;
1615–1712 in Derbyshire) b) Sunk chamfer (reserved chamfer) (1586–1675)
c) Chamfer and ovolo d) Sunk chamfer with convex planes (1638) e) Ovolo
(1567–1741) f) Ovolo and hollow
For examples see page 59–60.

39 – Mullions

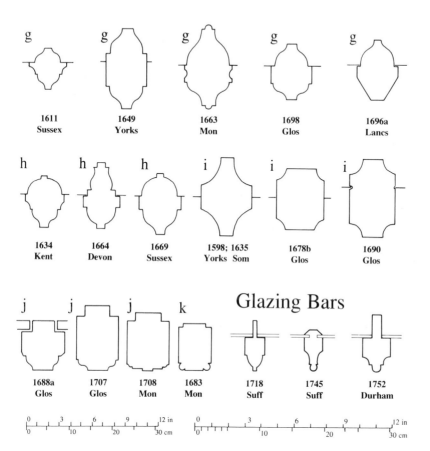

g
1611
Sussex

g
1649
Yorks

g
1663
Mon

g
1698
Glos

g
1696a
Lancs

h
1634
Kent

h
1664
Devon

h
1669
Sussex

i
1598; 1635
Yorks Som

i
1678b
Glos

i
1690
Glos

j
1688a
Glos

j
1707
Glos

j
1708
Mon

k
1683
Mon

Glazing Bars

1718
Suff

1745
Suff

1752
Durham

g) Ogee (1602–1678) h) Ogee and ovolo i) Hollow chamfer (cavetto)
(1582–1707) j) Internal small ogee with external rebate (1697–1739) k) Beaded:
very common but rarely recorded; date range uncertain
For examples see page 59–60.

40 – Overmantels

1570? Kent

1604 Suff

1655 Derbs

Other round-headed arches: 1602 Surrey; 1612 Sussex; 1616 Surrey; 1617 Surrey; 1621b Sussex; 1626 Sussex. Flattened arch: 1648 Yorks
Other geometric designs: 1602 Surrey; 1651 Yorks; 1656 Wilts; 1658 Northants; on panelling: 1636 Wilts; 1656 Surrey
Other Ionic capitals: 1602 Surrey; 1610 Sussex; 1617 Surrey; 1621b Sussex; 1626 Sussex; 1641 Sussex
Other carved wooden overmantels: 1622a Surrey; 1638 Flints

40

41 – Decoration

Arcading

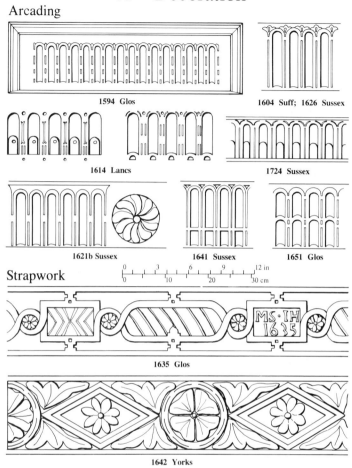

1594 Glos

1604 Suff; 1626 Sussex

1614 Lancs

1724 Sussex

1621b Sussex

1641 Sussex

1651 Glos

Strapwork

1635 Glos

1642 Yorks

Strapwork: 1604 Suff (p 40); 1634b Sussex (p 13); 1648 Lancs (p 7); 1674 Glos (p 47); 1678 Mon (p 13).
Lozenges: 1612 Sussex; 1623? Mon (p 16); 1625 Yorks; 1628 Westm; 1631 Wilts (p 46); 1636 Wilts (p 16); 1641 Sussex (p 16); 1651 Yorks; 1652 Yorks (p 16); 1656 Surrey; 1663 Glos (p 16); 1669 Glos (p 16); 1674 Glos (p 46); 1678b Yorks (p 47); 1692 Yorks (p.16); 1698 Lancs (p 47); 1698 Yorks (p 47)
Note: 1724 Sussex is the only 18th century example of arcading.

42 – Decoration

Lunettes

1570? Kent

1610 Sussex

1615 Angl

1615 Angl

1642 Glos

1621b Sussex

1661 Westm

1663 Mon

Guilloche

1661 Westm

1674 Glos

Lunettes: 1586 Som (p 15); 1628 Westm; 1664a Glos (p 49)
Guilloche: 1570 Flints; 1571 Flints (p 50); 1574 Merion; 1576/80 Caern; 1583
Denbs; 1585 Denbs; 1591 Denbs; 1597/1609 Surrey (p.7); 1602 Cambs; 1604
Suff (p 40); 1617 Surrey; 1617 Sussex; 1622a Surrey; 1634b Sussex; 1621b
Sussex; 1641 Sussex; 1678b Yorks; 1715 Westm

43 – Decoration

Double Scrolls

1625 Yorks

1626 Sussex

Scrolls

1648 Lancs

1649 Wilts

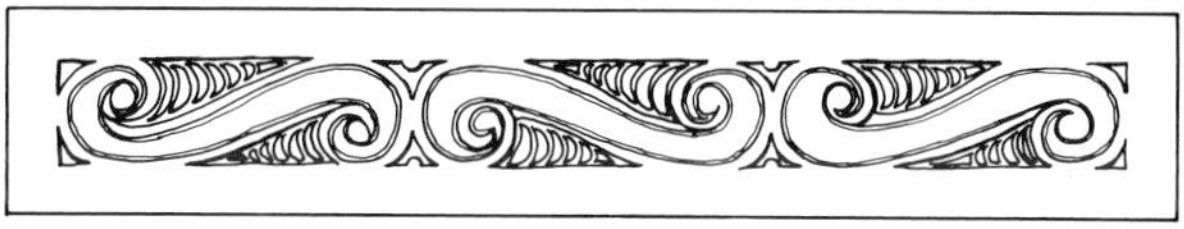

1651 Glos

1663 Mon

1702 Westm

Banded Decoration

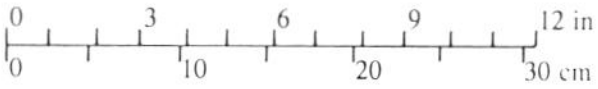

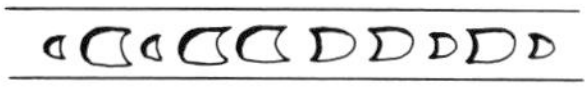

1674 Glos

1686b Glos

Double scroll (Heart): 1570? Kent; 1621b Sussex; 1628 Westm; 1651 Yorks; 1655 Derbs; 1661 Westm; 1678b Yorks (p 47); 1697 Westm; 1715 Westm
Scroll: 1612 Sussex; 1622a Surrey; 1625 Yorks; 1629 Westm; 1639 Yorks; 1648 Yorks; 1651 Yorks; 1661 Westm; 1664a Glos (p 49); 1674 Glos (p 47)

44 - Furniture

Dresser Ends

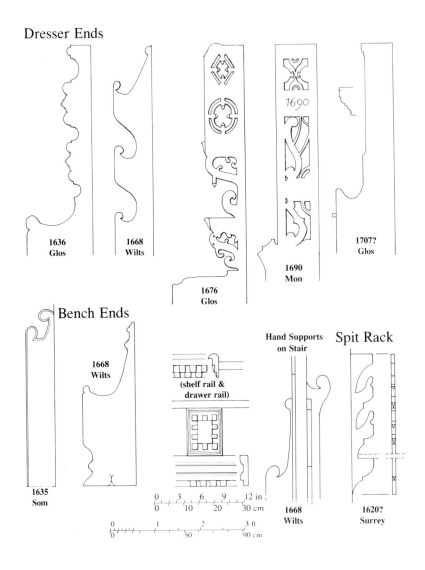

1636
Glos

1668
Wilts

1676
Glos

1690
Mon

1707?
Glos

Bench Ends

1668
Wilts

(shelf rail &
drawer rail)

1635
Som

**Hand Supports
on Stair**

Spit Rack

1668
Wilts

1620?
Surrey

0   3   6   9   12 in
0   10   20   30 cm

0   1   2   3 ft
0   50   90 cm

44

45 – Furniture

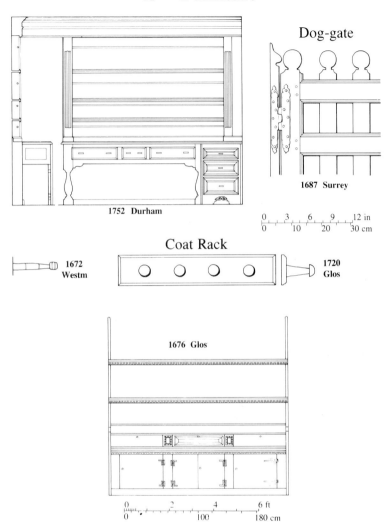

Dog-gate

1687 Surrey

1752 Durham

```
0      3      6      9    12 in
0        10      20      30 cm
```

Coat Rack

1672 Westm

1720 Glos

1676 Glos

```
0      2      4      6 ft
0            100      180 cm
```

Dressers with shelves only: 1636 Glos; 1668 Wilts
Dressers with shelves, drawers and cupboards: 1676 Glos; 1707? Glos; 1692 Devon
(plain ends); 1708 Wilts (carved ends, cornice and shelf brackets)
Other coat racks: 1697 Westm; 1702 Westm; 1743 Westm
Other dog-gates: 1659 Wilts; 1663/74 Westm; 1690 Flints; 1692 Yorks (solid
carved double gates); 1699 Oxon; 1702 Dorset; 1707 Norfolk

46 - Spice Cupboards

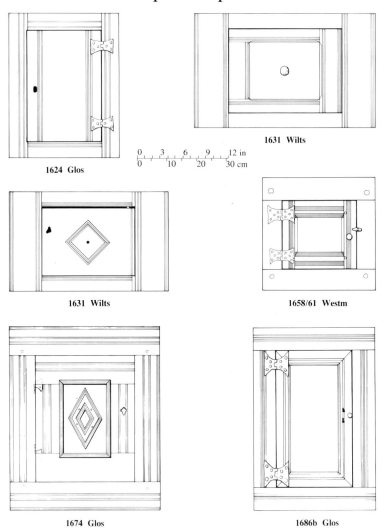

1624 Glos

1631 Wilts

1631 Wilts

1658/61 Westm

1674 Glos

1686b Glos

Spice cupboards mostly now have butterfly hinges, some replacing harr hanging, the door pivoting on wooden pegs set into the frame top and bottom (1631 Wilts) Scratch mouldings are commonly used on spice cupboards, doors and panelling (examples on page 60)

47 – Spice Cupboards

1674 Glos

0   3   6   9   12 in
0   10   20   30 cm

1698 Lancs

1678b Yorks

1698 Yorks

48 - Spice Cupboards

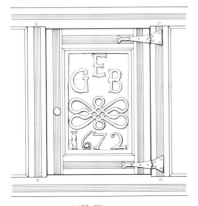

1672 Westm

1697 Westm

1681 Westm

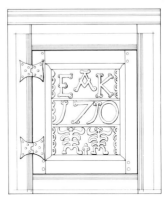

1710 Westm

48

49 – Spice Cupboards

1674 Westm

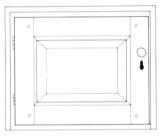

1752 Durham

1664a Glos

0   3   6   9   12 in
0   10   20   30 cm

50 - Panelling

Post & Panel

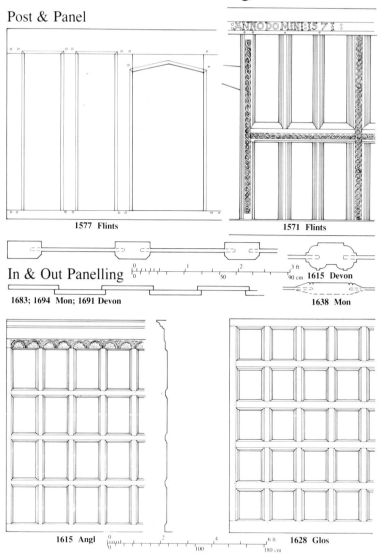

1577 Flints

1571 Flints

In & Out Panelling

1615 Devon

1683; 1694 Mon; 1691 Devon

1638 Mon

1615 Angl

1628 Glos

50

51 – Panelling

with Dado Rail

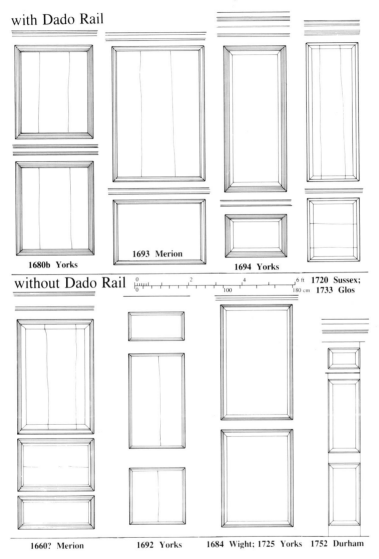

1680b Yorks

1693 Merion

1694 Yorks

without Dado Rail

0 ——————— 2 ——————— 4 ——————— 6 ft
0 ——————— 100 ——————— 180 cm

1720 Sussex;
1733 Glos

1660? Merion   1692 Yorks   1684 Wight; 1725 Yorks   1752 Durham

For examples see page 60

52 – Mouldings – Panelling

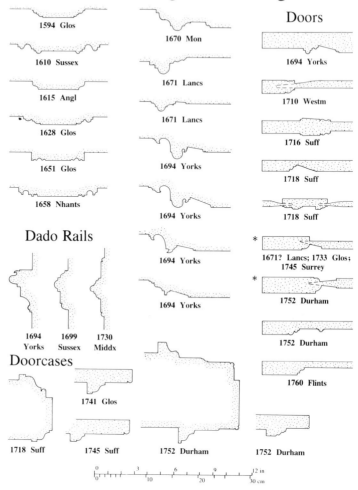

1594 Glos

1610 Sussex

1615 Angl

1628 Glos

1651 Glos

1658 Nhants

Dado Rails

1694 Yorks   1699 Sussex   1730 Middx

Doorcases

1741 Glos

1718 Suff   1745 Suff   1752 Durham   1752 Durham

1670 Mon

1671 Lancs

1671 Lancs

1694 Yorks

1694 Yorks

1694 Yorks

1694 Yorks

Doors

1694 Yorks

1710 Westm

1716 Suff

1718 Suff

1718 Suff

* 1671? Lancs; 1733 Glos; 1745 Surrey

* 1752 Durham

1752 Durham

1760 Flints

Other raised and fielded panels: 1660? Merion; 1694 Yorks; 1708 Yorks; 1710 Cambs; 1712 Surrey; 1720 Sussex; 1725 Sussex; 1725 Westm; 1725 Yorks; 1731 Devon; 1731 Sussex; 1739 Sussex; 1741 Glos; 1743 Westm; 1745 Surrey; 1752 Durham; 1754/5 Devon; 1757 Surrey; 1758 Sussex

53 – Mouldings – Doors

Door Fillets

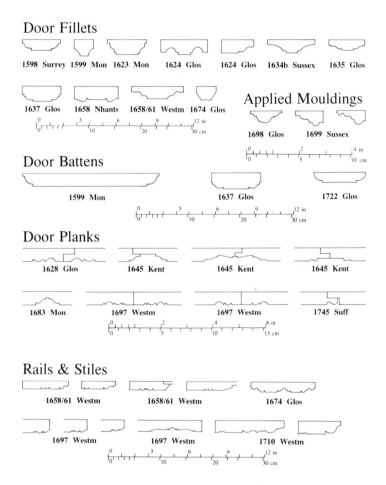

1598 Surrey   1599 Mon   1623 Mon   1624 Glos   1624 Glos   1634b Sussex   1635 Glos

1637 Glos   1658 Nhants   1658/61 Westm   1674 Glos

0   3   6   9   12 in
0   10   20   30 cm

Applied Mouldings

1698 Glos   1699 Sussex

0   2   4 in
0   5   10 cm

Door Battens

1599 Mon   1637 Glos   1722 Glos

0   3   6   9   12 in
0   10   20   30 cm

Door Planks

1628 Glos   1645 Kent   1645 Kent   1645 Kent

1683 Mon   1697 Westm   1697 Westm   1745 Suff

0   2   4   6 in
0   5   10   15 cm

Rails & Stiles

1658/61 Westm   1658/61 Westm   1674 Glos

1697 Westm   1697 Westm   1710 Westm

0   3   6   9   12 in
0   10   20   30 cm

54 – Mouldings

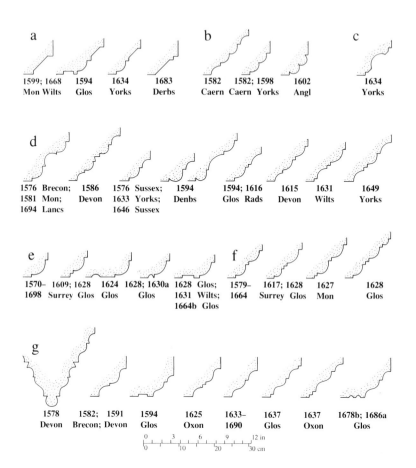

a) *Sunk chamfer (examples on stone fireplaces except 1599 Mon)* b) *Double roll*
c) *Hollow* d) *Hollow and ovolo* e) *Ovolo (1570–1698)* f) *Double ovolo*
(1579–1664) g) *Ogee and hollow (principally stone doorways or fireplaces)*
(1576–1690)
For examples see page 61

55 – Mouldings

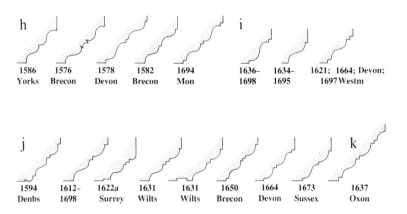

h					i		
1586 Yorks	1576 Brecon	1578 Devon	1582 Brecon	1694 Mon	1636– 1698	1634– 1695	1621; 1664; Devon; 1697 Westm

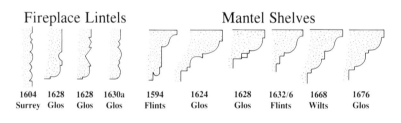

j								k
1594 Denbs	1612– 1698	1622a Surrey	1631 Wilts	1631 Wilts	1650 Brecon	1664 Devon	1673 Sussex	1637 Oxon

Fireplace Lintels   Mantel Shelves

1604 Surrey	1628 Glos	1628 Glos	1630a Glos	1594 Flints	1624 Glos	1628 Glos	1632/6 Flints	1668 Wilts	1676 Glos

h) Double ogee i) Ogee (cyma) (1634–1698) j) Ogee and ovolo (most are stone doorways or fireplaces, 1612–1698; also common in 18th century for cornices and mantelshelves; eg 1702 Sussex; 1720 Sussex)
For examples see page 61

56 – Mouldings

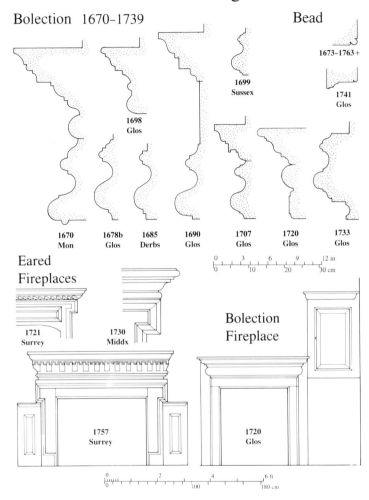

Bolection 1670–1739

Bead

1673–1763+

1699
Sussex

1741
Glos

1698
Glos

| 1670 | 1678b | 1685 | 1690 | 1707 | 1720 | 1733 |
| Mon | Glos | Derbs | Glos | Glos | Glos | Glos |

0   3   6   9   12 in
0   10   20   30 cm

Eared Fireplaces

1721
Surrey

1730
Middx

Bolection Fireplace

1757
Surrey

1720
Glos

0   2   4   6 ft
0   100   180 cm

Other bolection mouldings: 1691 Brecon; 1694 Yorks; 1698 Mon; 1702 Lancs; 1702 Sussex; 1707 Cumb; 1710 Cambs; 1739 Wilts
Bolection moulded bar below mantelshelf: 1698 Glos; 1720 Glos
Bead mouldings: 1673 Mon; 1683 Mon; 1687 Devon; 1691 Devon; 1720 Glos; 1722 Glos; 1723 Cornw; 1725 Sussex; 1725 Yorks; 1731 Sussex; 1736 Sussex; 1738 Sussex; 1739 Sussex; 1740 Oxon; 1741 Glos; 1745 Suff; 1763 Sussex
Eared fireplace surround: 1722 Glos

57 - Mouldings – Cornices

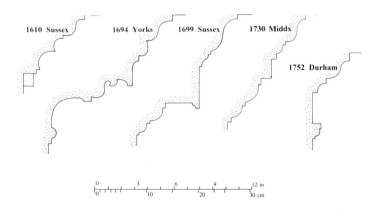

1610 Sussex

1694 Yorks

1699 Sussex

1730 Middx

1752 Durham

Additional Examples

13 — Stairs

13a *Open well stairs:* 1597/1609 Surrey; 1599 Kent; 1627 Mon; 1634b Sussex; 1635 Som; 1637 Oxon; 1641 Sussex; 1648 Lancs; 1656 Wilts; 1659 Wilts; 1678b Glos; 1683 Mon; 1691 Brecon; 1693 Brecon; 1698 Wilts; 1702 Sussex; 1707 Norf; 1714 Sussex; 1716 Suff; 1717 Sussex; 1720 Sussex; 1720 Yorks; 1721 Sussex; 1722 Glos; 1725 Flints; 1725 Sussex; 1733 Glos; 1744 Sussex

13b *Dog-leg stairs:* 1593 Sussex; 1624b Devon; 1627b Devon; 1628 Caern; 1633 Derbs; 1637 Glos; 1650 Brecon; 1656 Surrey; 1660 Merion; 1665 Devon; 1670 Brecon; 1673 Mon; 1676 Glos; 1678 Mon; 1687 Devon; 1693 Merion; 1698 Glos; 1700 Yorks; 1708 Yorks; 1717 Sussex; 1721 Westm; 1723 Surrey; 1725 Yorks; 1731 Devon; 1743 Surrey; 1743 Westm; 1744 Surrey; 1752 Durham; 1756 Lancs

13c *Closed well stairs:* 1582 Brecon; 1664b Glos

36 — Stops

36a *Runout:* 1607 Dorset; 1607 Wight; 1624 Derbs; 1651 Glos; 1657? Glos; 1675 Hants; 1697 Westm; 1707 Dorset; 1707 Glos

36c *Angled runout:* 1619 Mon; 1624 Derbs; 1630 Derbs; 1667 Derbs; 1642 Glos

36d *Straight cut (45°):* 1601 Mon; 1619 Mon

36g *Step:* 1571 Flints; 1583 Som; 1594 Denbs; 1594 Glos; 1601 Mon; 1604 Mon; 1607 Dorset; 1607 Mon; 1612 Sussex; 1615 Devon; 1616 Derbs; 1620 Surrey; 1625 Oxon; 1630b Glos; 1633 Mon; 1634 Devon; 1640 Mon; 1651 Surrey; 1652 Mon; 1656 Surrey; 1663 Mon; 1665 Dorset; 1667 Derbs; 1671 Mon; 1683 Mon; 1711 Rads; 1720 Wight; 1739 Devon

36i *Rounded step:* 1651 Surrey; 1656 Surrey

36l *Scroll:* 1591 Devon; 1594 Glos; 1604 Mon; 1607 Dorset; 1624 Derbs; 1624a Devon; 1624b Devon; 1624 Warws; 1627b Devon; 1630a Glos; 1630b Glos; 1633 Derbs; 1634b Sussex; 1634 Yorks; 1636 Rads; 1637 Som; 1638 Devon; 1648 Devon; 1650 Brecon; 1656 Surrey; 1664a Glos; 1664b Glos; 1668 Sussex; 1668 Wilts; 1669 Glos; 1672 Lancs; 1673 Staffs; 1674 Glos; 1675 Hants; 1677 Mont; 1678 Devon; 1678a Glos; 1678b Glos; 1685 Derbs; 1686b Glos; 1688a Glos; 1689 Surrey; 1695 Derbs; 1697 Westm; 1698 Glos; 1698 Lancs; 1722 Glos; 1726 Dorset; 1730 Surrey; 1731 Sussex; 1754/5 Devon; 1763 Sussex

36m *Scroll and flat:* 1623 Mon; 1637 Mon; 1669 Glos; 1678b Glos; 1686a Glos; 1688b Glos

36n *Scroll and bar:* 1638 Devon; 1655 Glos; 1683 Devon

36q *Scroll and step:* 1668 Wilts; 1698 Glos
36r *Scroll, bar, step and flat:* 1664 Devon
36s *Scroll and nick:* 1678 Devon; 1688a Glos; 1698 Glos

37 — Stops–Beams and Doorframes
37a *Bar:* 1583 Sussex; 1599 Sussex; 1600 Surrey; 1609 Surrey; 1614 Essex; 1622b Surrey; 1627b Devon; 1638 Devon; 1640 Mon; 1664 Devon; 1668 Sussex; 1673? Caern; 1679 Sussex; 1689 Leics. *Bar and nick:* 1664 Devon
37d *Bar and flat:* 1609 Surrey; 1625 Oxon; 1640 Mon; 1678b Glos
37h *Roll:* 1671/3 Mon; *Roll and flat:* 1678b Glos
37l *Converging:* 1616 Rads; 1624 Glos; 1628 Glos; 1630a Glos; 1630b Glos; 1633 Yorks; 1637 Glos; 1642? Flints; 1651 Glos; 1657? Glos; 1674 Glos; 1676 Glos; 1678b Glos; 1686a Glos; 1690 Glos; 1698 Glos; 1698 Lancs; *Converging with step:* 1582 Caern; *Converging with nick:* 1594 Denbs
37p *Keeled:* 1633 Mon
37q *Pyramid:* 1592 Glos; 1615 Angl
37r *Geometric:* 1630a Glos
37s *Shouldered step:* 1646 Sussex; 1674 Glos

38 — Mullions
38b *Sunk chamfer:* 1586/1600 Glam; 1601 Mon; 1605 Mon; 1606 Mon; 1607 Glam; 1611 Mon; 1613a Mon; 1619 Mon; 1631 Lancs; 1658 Glam; 1663 Mon; 1666 Rads; 1675 Mon
38d *Sunk chamfer with convex planes:* 1638 Mon
38e *Ovolo (1576–1682 East Sussex; 1594–1686 Glos; 1597–1741 Northants; 1605–1673 Mon; 1614–1691 Wilts; 1615–1694 Banbury region):* 1567 Wight; 1570? Kent; 1576 Sussex; 1580 Caern; 1581 Nhants; 1592 Lancs; 1593 Lancs; 1593 Sussex; 1594 Glos; 1594 Lancs; 1603? Lancs; 1604 Som; 1604 Sussex; 1612 Sussex; 1613b Mon; 1614 Wilts; 1615 Angl; 1615 Devon; 1615 Oxon; 1615 Wight; 1617 Lancs; 1621a Sussex; 1623 Mon; 1624 Som; 1627a Devon; 1627 Lancs; 1628 Glos; 1631 Wilts; 1633 Derbs; 1633 Lancs; 1634b Sussex; 1637 Som; 1638 Flints; 1639 Lancs; 1642 Glos; 1647 Oxon; 1651 Glos; 1653 Brecon; 1654 Nhants; 1655 Oxon; 1656 Oxon; 1656 Sussex; 1660 Nhants; 1663 Mon; 1664a Glos; 1664b Glos; 1668 Sussex; 1669 Glos; 1670 Brecon; 1671 Nhants; 1673 Mon; 1676 Glos; 1678a Glos; 1679 Wilts; 1680 Devon; 1682a Sussex; 1683 Derbs; 1686b Glos; 1694 Oxon; 1696b Lancs; 1717 Lancs

39 — Mullions
39g *Ogee:* 1602 Sussex; 1621b Sussex; 1634 Yorks; 1678a Yorks
39i *Hollow chamfer: (i) large:* 1577 Glos; 1582 Brecon; 1583 Denbs; 1590

Glos; 1598 Yorks; 1615 Oxon; 1631 Wilts; 1635 Som; 1636 Nhants; 1652 Angl; 1667 Derbs *(ii) small:* 1686a Glos *(iii) uncertain:* 1579 Lancs; 1600/1 Dorset; 1607 Dorset; 1617 Lancs; 1627 Lancs; 1636? Lancs; 1683 Wilts; 1707 Dorset

39j *Internal small ogee (presence of external rebate not always certain):* 1697 Wilts; 1702 Sussex; 1704 Wilts; 1717 Sussex; 1731 Sussex; 1739 Sussex

46 — Spice Cupboards
46a *Scratch mouldings on spice cupboards, doors and panelling:* 1624 Glos; 1625 Yorks; 1628 Glos; 1631 Wilts; 1639 Yorks; 1642 Glos; 1642 Yorks; 1651 Yorks; 1653 Yorks; 1655 Yorks; 1658/61 Westm; 1661a Yorks; 1664b Glos; 1669 Glos; 1672 Westm; 1674 Glos; 1678b Yorks; 1683 Mon; 1686b Glos; 1691 Devon; 1697 Westm; 1698 Yorks; 1710 Westm; 1727 Wight

50 — Panelling
50a *Post and panel (plank and muntin):* 1570 Flints; 1571 Flints; 1574 Merion; 1582 Brecon; 1593 Flints; 1607 Mon; 1620 Mont; 1625 Mon; 1627 Mon; 1628 Caern; 1632/6 Flints; 1637 Mon; 1638 Mon; 1640 Flints; 1650 Brecon; 1652 Mon; 1653 Brecon; 1658/61 Westm; 1680a Yorks; 1685 Caern; 1693 Merion; 1694 Mon; 1696 Devon; 1697 Westm; 1703 Mon; 1707 Dorset; 1719 Mont; 1725 Westm; 1743 Westm; 1745 Mon. Further examples in *Houses of the Welsh Countryside*
50b *Post and panel with middle rail (i) with guilloche decoration:* 1574 Merion; 1576 Caern; 1583 Denbs; 1585 Denbs; 1591 Denbs *(ii) others:* 1570 Flints; 1573/4 Denbs; 1619 Mon
50c *Small rectangular/square panels with moulded rails and muntins, four or five (occasionally six) panels high:* 1580 Caern; 1583 Yorks; 1594 Glos; 1597 Flints; 1604 Suff; 1612 Sussex; 1615 Angl; 1617 Surrey; 1621b Sussex; 1625 Yorks; 1626 Sussex; 1628 Glos; 1634b Sussex; 1638 Flints; 1641 Sussex; 1642 Glos; 1642 Yorks; 1648 Yorks; 1651 Yorks; 1663/74 Westm
50d *Three panels and frieze:* 1649 Wilts; 1658 Nhants; 1669 Glos

54–55 — Mouldings
54e *Ovolo:* 1570? Kent; 1576 Sussex; 1589 Oxon; 1593 Sussex; 1598 Yorks; 1604 Mon; 1604 Surrey; 1606 Devon; 1611 Sussex; 1613b Mon; 1615 Devon; 1617 Surrey; 1621b Sussex; 1623 Mon; 1624 Glos; 1624 Som; 1625 Oxon; 1627a Devon; 1627b Devon; 1628 Glos; 1631 Wilts; 1632 Devon; 1633 Derbs; 1633 Mon; 1634 Devon; 1634b Sussex; 1637 Glos; 1637 Mon; 1637 Som; 1638 Devon; 1638 Mon; 1642? Flints; 1651 Glos; 1656 Surrey; 1663 Devon; 1663 Mon; 1664 Devon; 1664a Glos; 1664b Glos; 1665 Devon; 1669 Glos; 1673 Mon; 1674 Glos; 1678a Glos; 1678b Glos; 1683

Mon; 1686a Glos; 1688a Glos; 1688b Glos; 1698 Glos; 1698 Lancs
54f *Double ovolo:* 1579 Sussex; 1602 Cambs; 1627 Mon; 1637 Mon; 1640 Mon; 1646 Sussex; 1664a Glos; 1669 Sussex; 1673 Sussex; 1674 Glos; 1634 Brecon (with double central fillet)
54g *Ogee and hollow:* 1576 Brecon; 1594 Glos; 1600/1 Dorset; 1607 Dorset; 1633 Derbs; 1676/8/9 Mon; 1678b Glos; 1679 Warws; 1686a Glos; 1690 Yorks;
55i *Ogee:* 1630 Derbs; 1634 Yorks; 1635 Som; 1636 Rads; 1637 Glos; 1649 Yorks; 1650 Brecon; 1651 Glos; 1657? Glos; 1659 Wilts; 1663 Mon; 1664 Devon; 1668 Wilts; 1669 Glos; 1674 Glos; 1676 Glos; 1678b Glos; 1683 Mon; 1686a Glos; 1689 Surrey; 1690 Glos; 1691 Yorks; 1695 Lancs; 1697 Westm; 1698 Glos
55j *Ogee and ovolo:* 1612 Sussex; 1624 Warws; 1631 Wilts; 1634 Kent; 1637 Som; 1649 Yorks; 1650 Yorks; 1664b Glos; 1668 Wilts; 1672 Lancs; 1673 Som; 1674 Glos; 1679 Mon; 1679 Wilts; 1690 Yorks; 1698 Glos

Gazetteer and Index

1591 Devon   SS595325 Acland Barton, Landkey: 14, 36, 36*l*, 54
1591 Surrey   TQ250503 6 Slipshoe Street, Reigate: 21, 22, 30
1592 Glos   ST600887 Link Farm, Elberton, Aust: 20, 35, 37*q*
1592 Lancs   SD810379 Lower Houses, Goldshaw Booth: 38*e*
1593 Flints   SJ279603 Fferm, Hope (also dated 1607): 50*a*
1593 Lancs   SD832403 Whitehough Grange, Bailey with Wheatley
                    Booth: 38*e*
1593 Sussex   TQ766190 Hancox, Whatlington: 8, 11, 13*b*, 38*e*, 54*e*
1594 Denbs   SJ065710 Perthewig, Trefnant: 36*g*, 37*l*, 54, 55
1594 Flints   SJ128747 Plas Cerrig, Caerwys: 55
1594 Glos   ST661915 Morton Grange, Thornbury: 20, 32, 33, 35,
                    36*g*, 36*l*, 38*e*, 41, 50*c*, 52, 54, 54*g*
1594 Lancs   SD821369 Ashlar House, Higham with West Close Booth:
                    38*e*
1597 Flints   SJ001764 Faenol Fawr, Bodelwyddan (cf. 1690, 1725):
                    50*c*
1597/1609 Surrey   TQ013696 Great Fosters, Egham (cf 1598): 1, 7, 8, 12,
                    13, 13*a*, 42
1597? Lancs   SD463528 Ware Cottage, Cockerham: 20
1598 Denbs   SH813565 Pentre-Mawr, Lanrwst Rural: 20
1598 Surrey   TQ013696 As 1597/1609: 15, 21, 30, 34, 53
1598 Yorks   SE044268 Peel House, Warley (cf 1691): 39, 39*i*, 54, 54*e*
1599 Kent   TQ735615 Great Kewlands, Burham: 1, 8, 11, 12, 13*a*
1599 Mon   SO411006 Allt-y-Bela, Langwm Ucha: 15, 20, 21, 22, 38,
                    53, 54
1599 Sussex   TQ723205 The Banks, Mountfield: 37*a*, 38
1600 Glam   ST009720 Beaupré, St Hilary (as 1586/1600): 35
1600 Surrey   TQ421510 Tenchley Manor, Limpsfield: 37*a*
1600/1 Dorset   ST596108 Gable Court, Yetminster: 39*i*, 54*g*
1601 Mon   ST426980 Trefella, Llangwm Ucha: 36*d*, 36*g*, 38*b*
1602 Angl   SH494777 Bodeilio, Llanddyfnan: 54
1602 Cambs   TL323562 Bourn Hall, Bourn: 42, 54*f*
1602 Devon   ST243045 Churchstyle, Stockland: 37
1602 Surrey   SU952412 Rake Manor, Witley: 40
1602 Sussex   TQ781236 Brasses, Ewhurst: 39*g*
1603? Lancs   SD878284 The Holme Briercliffe (cf 1717): 38*e*
1604 Mon   ST371908 Catsash, Langston: 36*g*, 36*l*, 54*e*
1604 Som   ST466132 High Cross, West Chinnock: 38*e*
1604 Suff   TL769449 Clare Priory, Clare: 40, 41, 42, 50*c*
1604 Surrey   TQ417501 Stockenden, Limpsfield: 14, 22, 27, 29, 35,
                    54*e*, 55

1604 Sussex	TQ771187 Spilsteads, Sedlescombe: 38*e*	
1605 Mon	SO421051 Treworgan, Llandenny: 38*b*	
1606 Devon	SS526417 Lower Aylescott Farm, West Down: 35, 54*e*	
1606 Mon	SO404244 Lower Dyffryn, Grosmont: 38*b*	
1607 Dorset	ST595108 Shop and Minster Cottage, Yetminster: 36*a*, 36*g*, 36*l*, 39*i*, 54*g*	
1607 Glam	SS908842 Maendy, St Bride's Minor: 38*b*	
1607 Mon	ST367939 Cefnhenllan, Tredunnock: 36*g*, 38, 50*a*	
1607 Wight	SZ427819 Marshgreen Farm, Brightstone: 36, 36*a*	
1608 Surrey	TQ142471 Old Cottage, Westcott: 37	
1609 Surrey	TQ142480 Old Manor House, St Martha, Chilworth: 1, 35, 37*a*, 37*d*, 54	
1610 Sussex	SU935219 Netherlands Farm, Tillington: 18, 22, 38, 40, 42, 52, 57	
1611 Mon	SO404244 The Shop, Grosmont: 38*b*	
1611 Sussex	TQ780180 1–5 Manor Cottages, Sedlescombe: 39, 54*e*	
1612 Sussex	TQ633297 Wenbans, Wadhurst: 35, 36*g*, 38*e*, 40, 41, 43, 50*c*, 55*j*	
1613a Mon	ST389999 Graig Olway, Llangeview: 38*b*	
1613b Mon	ST297933 Ty Coch, Llantarnam: 37, 38*e*, 54*e*	
1614 Essex	TL760240 Wentworth House, Bradford Street, Bocking: 37*a*	
1614 Lancs	SD354375 Fairfield Road, Hardhorn, Poulton-le-Fylde: 20, 41	
1614 Wilts	ST995585 Church House, 3 Rookes Lane, Potterne: 38*e*	
1615 Angl	SH465717 Plas Berw, Llanidan: 37*q*, 38, 38*e*, 42, 50, 50*c*, 52	
1615 Devon	SX649978 Halford Manor, Sampford Courtenay: 35, 36*g*, 38*e*, 50, 54, 54*e*	
1615 Oxon	SP416417 Wroxton Abbey, Wroxton: 38*e*, 39*i*	
1615 Wight	SZ521855 Merston Manor, Merston: 38*e*	
1616 Derbs	SK230542 Gate Inn, Brassington: 36*g*	
1616 Rads	SO313645 Radnorshire Arms, Presteigne: 37*l*, 54	
1616 Surrey	SU914477 Shoelands, Puttenham: 1, 13, 14, 21, 28, 30, 35, 40	
1617 Lancs	SD865365 Scholefield House, Nelson: 38*e*, 39*i*	
1617 Surrey	TQ393437 New Place, Lingfield: 37, 40, 42, 50*c*, 54, 54*e*	
1617 Sussex	TQ878187 Knellstone, Udimore: 11, 42	
1619 Mon	SO371190 Great Pool Hall, Llanvetherine (cf 1665): 36*c*, 36*d*, 38, 38*b*, 50*b*	

1620 Mont	SJ173187 Talwrn-bach, Llanfyllin: 50*a*
1620 Surrey	TQ073479 Elm Cottage, Shere: 31, 36*g*, 44
1620 Wight	SZ614860 Yaverland Manor, Yaverland: 8
1621 Devon	SX879803 Hams Barton, Chudleigh: 35, 55
1621a Sussex	TQ706290 Pashley, Ticehurst: 38*e*
1621b Sussex	TQ641301 Walland Manor, Wadhurst: 1, 8, 11, 19, 29, 35, 39*g*, 40, 41, 42, 43, 50*c*, 54*e*
1622a Surrey	TQ215499 More Place, Betchworth: 35, 40, 42, 43, 55
1622b Surrey	SU976443 Wyatts Almshouses, Godalming: 37*a*
1623 Mon	ST382926 Kemeys House, Kemeys Inferior, (also dated 1597): 11, 16, 23, 36*m*, 38*e*, 41, 53, 54*e*
1623 Surrey	SU998495 Abbott's Hospital, Guildford: 35
1624 Derbs	SK317755 Barlow Woodseats, Barlow: 36*a*, 36*c*, 36*l*
1624a Devon	SS567304 Tenement Farm, Bishop's Tawton: 36*l*
1624b Devon	SS516421 Manor House, Churchpool, West Down: 13*b*, 36*l*
1624 Glos	ST698764 Crump House, Pucklechurch: 8, 14, 15, 20, 21, 22, 24, 26, 27, 30, 37*l*, 38, 46, 46*a*, 53, 54, 54*e*, 55
1624 Som	ST627349 Corner House, Alhampton: 31, 33, 38*e*, 54*e*
1624 Warws	SP370813 Manor House (Farm), Wyken (SRJ): 36*l*, 55*j*
1625 Mon	ST408972 Nantybanw, Llantrisant: 38, 50*a*
1625 Oxon	SP377429 The Old Rectory, Alkerton (RWJ): 36*g*, 37*d*, 54, 54*e*
1625 Surrey	TQ312542 Willey Park Farm, Caterham: 14, 29, 35, 36
1625 Yorks	SE177294 439-443 Shetcliffe Lane, North Bierley: 24, 41, 43, 46*a*, 50*c*
1626 Sussex	TQ843236 Church House, Beckley (cf 1744): 40, 41, 43, 50*c*
1627a Devon	SY050851 Hayes Barton, East Budleigh: 38*e*, 54*e*
1627b Devon	SS385249 Fishleigh Barton, Tawstock: 13*b*, 24, 36*l*, 37*a*, 54*e*
1627 Lancs	SD876324 Jackson's Farm, Worsthorne: 38*e*, 39*i*
1627 Mon	SO462111 Treowen, Wonastow: 1, 13, 13*a*, 22, 23, 50*a*, 54, 54*f*
1627 Wilts	ST869690 Great Lypiatt Farm, Corsham: 1
1628 Caern	SH314297 Castellmarch, Llanengan: 5, 8, 13, 13*b*, 50*a*
1628 Glos	ST637880 Street Farm, Alveston: 1, 8, 10, 14, 20, 21, 24, 25, 27, 29, 36, 37, 37*l*, 38*e*, 46*a*, 50, 50*c*, 52, 53, 54, 54*e*, 55
1628 Westm	SD422996 Common Farm, Windermere (cf 1715, 1721):

	41, 42, 43
1629 Westm	NY384186 Glencoyne Farm, Patterdale: 22, 29, 43
1630 Derbs	SK208642 Old Hall Farm, Youlgreave: 36*c*, 55*i*
1630a Glos	ST655854 Whitehouse Farm, Alveston: 20, 36, 36*l*, 37, 37*l*, 37*r*, 54, 55
1630b Glos	ST654807 Hick's Farm, Winterbourne: 14, 20, 21, 26, 36*g*, 36*l*, 37*l*
1631 Lancs	SD873313 Higher Red Lees, Briercliffe: 38*b*
1631 Wilts	ST915624 Woolmore Farm, Melksham: 18, 35, 38*e*, 39*i*, 41, 46, 46*a*, 54, 54*e*, 55, 55*j*
1632 Devon	SS555462 Hill Barton, Berrynarbor: 54*e*
1632/6 Flints	SJ062779 Pentre, Cwm: 20, 50*a*, 55
1633 Derbs	SK310591 Riber Manor, Riber: 13*b*, 25, 36*l*, 38*e*, 54*e*, 54*g*
1633 Lancs	SD874324 Worsthorne Hall, Worsthorne: 38*e*
1633 Mon	ST326965 Glebe Farm, Llandegveth: 20, 36*g*, 37*p*, 54*e*
1633 Yorks	SD766659 Middle Birks, Clapham and Newby: 37*l*, 54
1634 Brecon	SO257202 Dyffryn, Llanbedr Ystrad Yw: 20, 27, 54*f*
1634 Devon	SX780624 Knoddy, Dartington: 36, 36*g*, 54*e*
1634 Kent	TQ767357 Goddards Green, Cranbrook: 39, 55*j*
1634a Sussex	TQ001143 Cross Street Farm, West Burton: 15, 21, 27, 28, 30
1634b Sussex	TQ671238 Batemans, Burwash: 1, 8, 13, 13*a*, 14, 15, 23, 27, 28, 30, 34, 35, 36*l*, 38*e*, 41, 42, 50*c*, 53, 54*e*
1634 Yorks	SE079229 Lower Old Hall, Norland: 36*l*, 39*g*, 54, 55*i*
1635 Glos	SP023020 Town Hall, Cirencester: 21, 34, 41, 53
1635 Som	ST230244 Grays Almshouses, Taunton: 1, 8, 11, 13*a*, 24, 35, 39, 39*i*, 44, 55*i*
1636 Glos	ST712798 Church Farm, Wapley, Dodington: 44, 45
1636 Nhants	SP555454 Dial House, Sulgrave (RWJ): 39*i*
1636 Rads	SO204785 Bryndraenog, Bugeildy: 36*l*, 55*i*
1636 Wilts	ST826567 Church Farm, Wingfield: 14, 16, 23, 30, 40, 41
1636? Lancs	SD878370 Southfield Fold Farm, Southfield, Nelson: 39*i*
1637 Glos	ST571816 Manor Farm, Compton Greenfield, Almondsbury: 13*b*, 16, 21, 22, 26, 30, 31, 32, 34, 37*l*, 38, 53, 54, 54*e*, 55*i*
1637 Mon	SO357138 Cefn Gwyn, Llanddewi Rhydderch: 20, 36, 36*m*, 38, 50*a*, 54*e*, 54*f*
1637 Oxon	SP515062 130a High Street, Oxford: 5, 7, 8, 13, 13*a*, 35, 38, 54, 55
1637 Som	ST492134 Weston House, East Chinnock: 36*l*, 38*e*, 54*e*,

1638 Devon	SS571272 Wick Farm, Tawstock: 36*l*, 36*n*, 37*a*, 54*e*
1638 Flints	SJ241600 Nercwys Hall, Nercwys: 38*e*, 40, 50*c*
1638 Mon	SO401253 Kingsfield, Grosmont: 23, 36, 38*d*, 50, 50*a*, 54*e*
1639 Lancs	SD784323 Shuttleworth Hall, Hapton: 38*e*
1639 Yorks	SE193532 Swinsty Hall, Fewston, Harrogate: 1, 10, 18, 24, 25, 43, 46*a*
1640 Flints	SJ249624 Pentrehobyn, Mold Rural: 50*a*
1640 Mon	SO438099 Ty-mawr, Dingestow: 36*g*, 37, 37*a*, 37*d*, 54*f*
1641 Sussex	TQ760273 Great Wigsell, Salehurst: 1, 8, 13, 13*a*, 16, 27, 40, 41, 42, 50*c*
1642? Flints	SJ179629 Brithdir-mawr, Cilcain: 37*l*, 54*e*
1642 Glos	ST686821 309 & 311 Badminton Road, Mayshill, Westerleigh: 15, 20, 21, 24, 26, 36, 36*c*, 37, 38*e*, 42, 46*a*, 50*c*
1642 Yorks	SE058194 Howroyd, Barkisland: 1, 41, 46*a*, 50*c*
1645 Kent	TR166623 Vale Farmhouse, Broadoak, Sturry: 26, 31, 32, 53
1645 Surrey	TQ107597 Mole Cottage, Cobham: 36
1646 London	TQ333815 9 Great St Helen's, Bishopsgate (V & A Cat. 154–1892): 5, 8, 12, 13
1646 Sussex	TQ004308 Todhurst, Plaistow: 35, 37*s*, 38, 54, 54*f*
1647 Oxon	SP480318 Castle End, Deddington (RWJ): 38*e*
1648 Devon	SY135985 Crabbs Cottage, Gittisham: 36*l*
1648 Lancs	SD724116 Hall i th'Wood, Bolton: 1, 7, 12, 13, 13*a*, 14, 23, 41, 43
1648 Yorks	SE078420 East Riddlesdon Hall, Morton: 40, 43, 50*c*
1648/9 Wilts	ST811692 Coles Farm, Box: 10, 35
1649 Brecon	SO281223 Tyn-y-Llyn, Partrisio: 20
1649 Wilts	ST811692 As 1648/9: 43, 50*d*
1649 Yorks	SE043236 Wood Lane Hall, Sowerby: 1, 10, 18, 39, 54, 55*i*, 55*j*
1650 Brecon	SO220398 Penyrwrlod, Llanigon: 13*b*, 36*l*, 50*a*, 55, 55*i*
1650 Yorks	SE039254 Kershaw House, Midgley: 55*j*
1651 Glos	ST698765 Church Farm, Pucklechurch: 24, 35, 36*a*, 37, 37*l*, 38*e*, 41, 43, 52, 54*e*, 55*i*
1651 Surrey	TQ279429 Ringley Oak Cottage, Horley: 36*g*, 36*i*
1651 Yorks	SE206267 Peel House, Gomershal: 40, 41, 43, 46*a*, 50*c*
1652 Angl	SH380667 Bodowen, Llangadwaladr: 39*i*

1652 Mon	ST395952 Llywnau, Llantrissent: 36g, 50a
1652 Sussex	SU977216 Dawtrey Mansion, Petworth: 12, 13
1652 Yorks	SE305252 East Ardsley Hall, Marley: 16, 41
1653 Brecon	SO128299 Trewalter, Llan-gors: 36, 38e, 50a
1653 Wilts	SU188694 6-7 Kingsbury Street, Marlborough: 6, 11
1653 Yorks	SE101734 Holme Farm, Lofthouse: 1, 8, 46a
1654 Leics	SP712946 House, Tur Langton (SRJ): 36
1654 Nhants	SP494446 Poplars Farm, Chacombe (RWJ): 38, 38e
1655 Derbs	SK305329 Mickleover Old Hall, Mickleover: 40, 43
1655 Glos	ST700809 Rodford Cottages, Westerleigh: 36n
1655 Oxon	SP480318 School House, Deddington, (Hopcroft Lane) (RWJ): 38e
1655 Yorks	SE506297 Manor House, Monk Fryston: 18, 46a
1656 Oxon	SP473356 The Rookery, Adderbury East (RWJ): 38e
1656 Surrey	SU956617 Brook Place, West End, Chobham: 8, 11, 13b, 19, 25, 29, 35, 36, 36g, 36i, 36l, 38, 40, 41, 54e
1656 Sussex	TQ817125 Great Ridge, Ore: 38e
1656 Wilts	SU187691 132 High Street, Marlborough: 1, 7, 13a, 18, 40
1657? Glos	ST604829 Upper Hempton Farm, Almondsbury: 22, 35, 36a, 37, 37l, 38, 55i
1658 Glam	ST011753 Ty-Mawr, Aberthin: 38b
1658 Nhants	SP488404 Warkworth Farm, Warkworth (RWJ): 50d, 52, 53
1658/61 Westm	NY415001 Causeway Farm, Windermere: 14, 16, 22, 24, 27, 28, 29, 30, 46, 46a, 50a, 53
1659 Wilts	ST865763 Manor Farm, Yatton Keynell: 5, 6, 12, 13a, 28, 35, 45, 55i
1660 Merion	SH600231 Corsygedol, Llanddwywe-is-y-Graig: 2, 12, 13b, 51, 52
1660 Nhants	SP484524 Manor House, Lower Boddington (RWJ): 38e
1661 Westm	NY415001 As 1658/61: 24, 42, 43
1661a Yorks	SE227632 Brimham Lodge, Hartwith: 18, 46a
1661b Yorks	SE257189 Combs Hall Farm, Thornhill: 6, 10
1663 Devon	SS492320 Chapple Farm, Fremington: 35, 54e
1663 Glos	ST59 74 House, Montpelier, Bristol (1913 drg Bristol City Mus, S. Loxton): 6, 11, 16, 41
1663 Mon	ST365958 Ton, Llangibby: 22, 36, 36g, 37, 38b, 38e, 39, 42, 43, 54e, 55i
1663/74 Westm	SD508918 Collinfield Manor, Kendal: 6, 45, 49, 50c

68

1664 Devon	SX878514 4 The Quay, Dartmouth: 36, 36r, 37a, 39, 54e, 55, 55i
1664a Glos	ST726904 South End House, Charfield: 22, 27, 35, 36l, 38e, 42, 43, 49, 54e, 54f
1664b Glos	ST686826 Rangeworthy Court, Rangeworthy: 13c, 22, 27, 32, 35, 36l, 38e, 46a, 54, 54e, 55j
1664 Yorks	SE073231 Lower Wat Ing, Norland: 18
1665 Devon	SS511373 Ash Barton, Braunton: 10, 13b, 35, 54e
1665 Dorset	ST622077 Rookery Farm, Leigh, Yetminster: 36g
1665 Mon	SO371190 Great Pool Hall, Llanvetherine (cf 1619): 2
1665 Sussex	TQ689145 Ashburnham Place, Ashburnham: 2, 11, 27, 28, 34
1666 Rads	SO301710 Farrington, Knighton: 38b
1666 Surrey	TQ147416 Mearshurst, Ockley: 22, 29, 31
1666 Yorks	SE226604 Hardcastle Garth, Hartwith cum Winsley: 23
1667 Derbs	SK303608 Wellfield Cottage, Matlock: 36c, 36g, 39i
1668 Nhants	SP497421 Springfield House, Middleton Cheney (RWJ): 6, 11
1668 Sussex	TQ788190 Hurst House, Sedlescombe: 36l, 37a, 38e
1668 Wilts	ST872701 Hungerford Almshouses, Corsham: 5, 10, 35, 36l, 36q, 44, 45, 54, 55, 55i, 55j
1669 Glos	ST699905 The Gables, Cromhall: 16, 17, 20, 22, 24, 26, 27, 34, 36l, 36m, 38e, 41, 46a, 50d, 54e, 55i
1669 Sussex	TQ750158 The Deanery, Battle: 14, 16, 22, 30, 35, 39, 54f
1669 Yorks	SE201306 Ryecroft, Tong: 2, 10
1670 Brecon	SO082424 Pool Hall, Crucadarn: 13b, 38e
1670 Cornw	SW384355 Pendeen, St Just in Penwith: 35
1670 Mon	SO421051 Treworgan, Llandenny: 52, 56
1670 Yorks	SE119209 New Hall, Elland: 2
1671 Lancs	SD414398 Little Eccleston Hall, Little Eccleston: 8, 10, 52
1671 Mon	ST427999 Pwll, Llangwm Ucha: 23, 36g
1671 Nhants	SP513333 Old Grammar School, Aynho (RWJ): 38e
1671/3 Mon	SO403243 Town Farm, Grosmont: 37h
1672 Lancs	SD503648 Townend, Halton: 36l, 55j
1672 Westm	NY407022 Townend, Troutbeck (cf 1702): 24, 45, 46a, 48
1673 Mon	SO507129 Castle House, Monmouth: 4, 12, 13, 13b, 20, 23, 38, 38e, 54e, 56

1673 Som	ST467135 Manor Farm, West Chinnock: 31, 55*j*
1673 Staffs	SP924141 House, Penkridge (SRJ): 36*l*
1673 Sussex	TQ784160 Chant Stream Cottage, Westfield: 54*f*, 55
1673? Caern	SH802807 Gloddaeth, Penrhyn: 37*a*
1674 Glos	ST709866 Hallend Farm, Yate: 14, 15, 16, 17, 20, 22, 24, 27, 29, 30, 34, 35, 36, 36*l*, 37*l*, 37*s*, 41, 42, 43, 46, 46*a*, 47, 53, 54*e*, 54*f*, 55*i*, 55*j*
1674 Westm	SD508918 As 1663/74: 49
1675 Hants	SU775299 Goleigh Farm, Greatham: 36*a*, 36*l*
1675 Mon	SO409121 High House, Penrhos: 7, 38*b*
1676 Derbs	SK216765 Eyam Hall, Eyam: 2, 10, 11, 12
1676 Glos	ST652789 Moorend Farm, Hambrook, Winterbourne: 2, 13*b*, 14, 19, 20, 22, 23, 24, 26, 27, 28, 30, 32, 34, 37*l*, 38*e*, 44, 45, 55, 55*i*
1676 Lancs	SD527545 Greenbank House, Abbey Mead, Lancaster: 2, 8, 11
1676 Westm	SD659177 Barwise Hall, Appleby: 2, 10
1676/8/9 Mon	SO423097 Artha, Tregaer: 54*g*
1677 Mon	SN978917 Ffinnant, Trefeglwys: 36*l*
1677 Yorks	SE082479 3 Fir Cottage, Addingham: 21
1678 Devon	ST279032 Nimrods, Membury: 36*l*, 36*s*
1678a Glos	ST575847 Rookery Farm, Pilning: 2, 8, 19, 25, 33, 36*l*, 37, 38*e*, 54*e*
1678b Glos	ST696766 Grey House, Pucklechurch: 4, 7, 8, 10, 12, 13*a*, 35, 36*l*, 36*m*, 37*d*, 37*h*, 37*l*, 39, 54, 54*e*, 54*g*, 55*i*, 56
1678 Mon	SO423097 As 1676/8/9: 6, 13, 13*b*, 41
1678a Yorks	SD821650 The Manor House, Langcliffe: 18, 24, 39*g*
1678b Yorks	SE696866 14 High Market Place, Kirbymoorside: 41, 42, 43, 46*a*, 47
1679 Mon	SO423097 As 1676/8/9: 55*j*
1679 Sussex	TQ760134 Blacklands, Crowhurst: 37*a*
1679 Warws	SP412502 The Old House, Avon Dassett (RWJ): 37, 54*g*
1679 Wilts	ST882757 Fowlswick Farm, Allington: 36, 38*e*, 55*j*
1680 Devon	SX788811 Wreyland Manor, Lustleigh: 38*e*
1680a Yorks	SE203605 Manor Farm, Hartwith cum Winsley: 50*a*
1680b Yorks	SE341221 Clarke Hall, Stanley: 6, 10, 11, 12, 25, 51
1681 Westm	SD431992 Heaning Farm, Windermere: 48
1682a Sussex	TQ722265 Haremere Hall, Etchingham: 4, 7, 8, 10, 38*e*
1682b Sussex	TQ783095 Filsham Farm, Hastings: 2, 8, 11
1683 Derbs	SK266501 Barley Mow, Kirk Ireton: 38*e*, 54

1683 Devon	ST258069 Moxhayes, Membury: 23, 36*n*, 37	
1683 Mon	SO472063 Pentre Wylan, Cwmcarvan: 2, 8, 11, 13*a*, 36*g*, 39, 46*a*, 50, 53, 54*e*, 55*i*, 56	
1683 Wilts	ST997713 3 Market Hill, Calne: 39*i*	
1683/4 Wight	SZ395856 Shalcombe Manor, Shalcombe: 6, 8, 10	
1684 Wight	SZ395856 As 1683/4: 17, 25, 51	
1685 Caern	SH805505 Parc, Penmachno: 50*a*	
1685 Derbs	SK339649 Hardwick Farm, Ashover: 36*l*, 56	
1685 Essex	TL867295 Colneford House, White Colne: 2, 11, 19, 32	
1685 Oxon	SP455457 Friar's Cottage, Great Bourton (SRJ) (RWJ): 36	
1686 Derbs	SK228574 Green Farm, Aldwark: 36	
1686a Glos	ST663845 Commonwealth House, Latteridge, Iron Acton: 5, 7, 8, 10, 33, 36*m*, 37*l*, 39*i*, 54, 54*e*, 54*g*, 55*i*	
1686b Glos	ST698796 The Old Stores, Westerleigh: 17, 27, 36*l*, 38*e*, 43, 46, 46*a*	
1687 Devon	SS510438 Twitchen Farm, West Down: 13*b*, 56	
1687 Surrey	TQ009363 Pound Farm, Dunsfold: 2, 25, 28, 45	
1687 Sussex	TQ782179 Harriet House, Sedlescombe: 31	
1688a Glos	ST683835 The Nook, Iron Acton: 24, 36*l*, 36*s*, 39, 54*e*	
1688b Glos	ST712872 Hall End Farm, Yate: 17, 36*m*, 54*e*	
1689 Leics	SP798930 Saddler's Cottage, Medbourne (SRJ): 20, 37*a*, 38	
1689 Surrey	SU933478 58 The Street, Puttenham: 10, 36*l*, 37, 55*i*	
1690 Flints	SJ001764 Faenol Fawr, Bodelwyddan (cf 1597, 1725): 5, 6, 10, 12, 45	
1690 Glos	ST681835 Lamb Inn, Iron Acton: 37, 37*l*, 39, 55*i*, 56	
1690 Mon	ST465983 Lower Kilgwrrwg, Kilgwrrwg: 11, 44	
1690 Warws	SP380807 Walsgrave Hall, outbuildings, Walsgrave-on-Sowe (dem.) (SRJ): 37	
1690 Yorks	SE069233 Upper Hall, Norland: 54*g*, 55*j*	
1691 Brecon	SO107251 Sgethrog, Llansanffraid: 13*a*, 56	
1691 Devon	ST201055 Underdown, Yarcombe: 24, 25, 46*a*, 50, 56	
1691 Wilts	SU034730 Manor House, Compton Bassett: 4	
1691 Yorks	SE044268 Peel House, Warley (cf 1598): 55*i*	
1692 Devon	SS455265 28 Bridgeland Street, Bideford: 25, 45	
1692 Essex	TL522345 Crown House, Newport: 4, 8, 11	
1692 Sussex	TQ894239 Forstall, Iden: 10	
1692 Yorks	SE13 25 Langley House, Hipperholme: 2, 11, 12, 16, 26, 41, 45, 51	

1693 Brecon	SO233139 Clydah House, Llanelli: 4, 13*a*
1693 Merion	SH699430 Pengwern, Ffestiniog: 4, 13*b*, 17, 50*a*, 51
1694 Lancs	SD603675 Church House, Wray: 54
1694 Mon	SO284274 Cwmbwchel, Upper Cwmyoy: 20, 50, 50*a*, 55
1694 Oxon	SU48 92 House, Milton: 38*e*
1694 Yorks	SE369343 Austhorpe Hall, Austhorpe: 25, 51, 52, 56, 57
1695 Derbs	SK207501 Brook House, Kniveton: 36*l*
1695 Lancs	SD503649 Manor House, Halton: 55*i*
1696 Devon	SX715875 Great Weeke Farm Cottage, Chudleigh: 50*a*
1696a Lancs	SD858396 Bank Hall, Barrowford Booth: 39
1696b Lancs	SD846315 Huffling Hall, Huffling Lane, Habergham Eaves: 38*e*
1697 Westm	NY332017 High Arnside Farm, Skelwith: 29, 36*a*, 36*l*, 43, 45, 46*a*, 48, 50*a*, 53, 55, 55*i*
1697 Wilts	ST824608 9A Church Street, Bradford-on-Avon: 39*j*
1698 Glos	ST638788 Faber's Farm, Hambrook, Winterbourne: 2, 7, 8, 10, 12, 13*b*, 20, 22, 25, 26, 31, 32, 35, 36*l*, 36*q*, 36*s*, 37*l*, 39, 53, 54*e*, 55*i*, 55*j*, 56
1698 Lancs	SD504363 Moons Farm, Hollowforth: 17, 22, 29, 36*l*, 37*l*, 41, 47, 54*e*
1698 Mon	SO306171 Great House, Llantilio Pertholey: 56
1698 Wilts	SU163606 Buckleaze Farm, Pewsey: 2, 8, 11, 13*a*
1698 Yorks	SE082476 Cragg House, Addingham: 24, 41, 46*a*, 47
1699 Essex	TL701257 Great Saling Hall, Great Saling: 33
1699 Oxon	SP480455 Home Farm, Williamscot: 45
1699 Sussex	TQ676248 Rampyndene, Burwash: 2, 7, 8, 11, 12, 17, 25, 31, 33, 52, 53, 56, 57
1700 Yorks	SE223264 Birstall Old Hall, Birstall, Batley: 6, 10, 13*b*
1701 Wight	SZ499891 God's Providence House, Newport: 4, 11, 12, 17
1702 Dorset	ST609066 Withyhook Mill, Leigh, Yetminster: 45
1702 Lancs	SD896398 Carrybridge Hall, Colne: 56
1702 Sussex	TQ692128 Lower Standard Hill, Ninfield: 3, 8, 11, 12, 13*a*, 39*j*, 55, 56
1702 Westm	NY407022 Townend, Troutbeck: 43, 45
1703 Mon	ST391968 Church Farm, Llantrisant: 50*a*
1704 Wilts	ST829613 1–5 New Road, Bradford-on-Avon: 39*j*
1707 Cumb	NY328591 Burgh Head Farmhouse, Burgh-by-Sands: 56
1707 Dorset	ST596109 Lower Farm, Yetminster: 36*a*, 39*i*, 50*a*
1707 Glos	ST561864 Northwick House Farm, Pilning: 19, 24, 25,

26, 28, 30, 31, 33, 36, 36*a*, 39, 44, 45, 56

1707 Norf	TG146309 Manor Farm, Itteringham: 4, 9, 13*a*, 45
1708 Mon	SO314106 Glan-usk, Llanelen: 39
1708 Wilts	SU099935 23 High Street, Cricklade: 45
1708 Yorks	SE401148 Newstead Hall, Havecroft: 3, 8, 9, 10, 12, 13*b*, 17, 52
1709 Westm	NY445918 Spout Farm, Crosthwaite: 3
1710 Cambs	TL564662 Tetworth Hall, Gamlingay: 4, 9, 52, 56
1710 Westm	NY365064 Rydal Mount, Rydal: 24, 46*a*, 48, 52, 53
1711 Rads	SO013781 Prysgduon, Abbey Cwm-hir: 36*g*
1712 Surrey	TQ161493 Clarendon House, Dorking: 3, 18, 19, 52
1713 Cambs	TL218531 House, Reach: 6
1713 Glos	ST603841 Almondsbury Church: 22, 26, 28, 30, 34
1714 Sussex	TQ864191 Pound Farm, Udimore: 3, 7, 8, 13*a*
1715 Westm	SD422996 Common Farm, Windermere (cf 1628, 1721): 42, 43
1716 Suff	TM085551 House, High Street, Needham Market: 3, 8, 10, 13*a*, 17, 21, 25, 33, 34, 52
1716 Yorks	SE315189 Lupsett Hall, Alverthorpe: 9
1717 Lancs	SD878284 The Holme Briercliffe (cf 1603): 38*e*
1717 Sussex	TQ649174 Little Bucksteep, Warbleton: 3, 7, 8, 11, 13*a*, 13*b*, 39*j*
1718 London	TQ273777 6 Cheyne Walk, Chelsea: 4
1718 Suff	TM084552 House, High Street, Needham Market: 24, 25, 26, 39, 52
1719 Mont	SH901051 Plas Rhiwsaeson, Llanbrynmawr: 50*a*
1720 Glos	SO903056 Rose Hill Cottage, Bisley: 31, 45, 56
1720 Sussex	TQ615179 Kingsley Hill House, Warbleton: 3, 8, 9, 13*a*, 17, 26, 51, 52, 55
1720 Wight	SZ484819 West Billingham Farm, Chillerton (Shorwell?): 33, 36*g*
1720 Yorks	SE366306 Lawns Farm, Newsam Green, Temple Newsam, Leeds: 6, 13*a*
1721 Surrey	SU906327 Collards, Petworth Road, Haslemere: 25, 28, 32, 33, 56
1721 Sussex	TQ663114 White Friars, Wartling: 3, 9, 13*a*, 31, 33
1721 Westm	SD422996 Common Farm, Windermere (cf 1628, 1715): 13*b*, 25
1722 Glos	ST722859 Oxwick Farm, Yate: 3, 8, 13*a*, 14, 18, 21, 22, 26, 28, 34, 36*l*, 53, 56

1723 Cornw	SW703217 Tredgadra, Mawgan-in-Meneage: 6, 56
1723 Surrey	TQ043670 Curfew House (12 Windsor Street), Chertsey: 13*b*
1724 Sussex	TQ608160 Cralle, Warbleton: 3, 8, 9, 41
1725 Flints	SJ001764 Faenol Fawr, Bodelwyddan (cf 1597, 1690): 3, 9, 13*a*
1725 Sussex	TQ777255 Newhouse, Bodiam: 3, 7, 8, 13*a*, 24, 25, 52, 56
1725 Westm	NY283055 Wall End Farm, Langdale: 26, 50*a*, 52
1725 Yorks	SE312151 Hollingthorpe Farm, Crigglestone: 3, 11, 13*b*, 17, 51, 52, 56
1726 Dorset	ST620086 Cromwell Cottage, Leigh, Yetminster: 36*l*
1727 Oxon	SP387333 Dolphin Inn, Wigginton: 31, 32, 37
1727 Wight	SZ508841 The Bays, Rookley: 19, 24, 25, 46*a*
1729 Surrey	TQ198421 Dean House Farm, Newdigate: 29
1730 Middx	TQ052688 Dial House, Laleham: 12, 24, 27, 52, 56, 57
1730 Surrey	TQ144486 Ivy Cottage, Westcott: 25, 32, 36, 36*l*
1731 Devon	SS656324 South Stoodleigh Farm, East and West Buckland: 9, 13*b*, 52
1731 Sussex	TQ619145 Cowbeech House, Herstmonceux: 3, 4, 8, 9, 25, 36*l*, 39*j*, 52, 56
1733 Glos	ST667817 Step House, Frampton Cotterell: 3, 8, 9, 13*a*, 22, 51, 52, 56
1734 Sussex	TQ613179 Old Rectory, Warbleton: 31
1736 Sussex	TQ781224 Cross Inn, Ewhurst: 56
1738 Sussex	TQ781178 Homestall, Sedlescombe: 56
1738 Yorks	SE315711 Old Hall, Ripon: 3
1739 Devon	SS666451 East Bodley Farm, Parracombe (cf 1754/5): 36*g*
1739 Sussex	TQ609182 Old Church House, Warbleton: 39*j*, 52, 56
1739 Wilts	ST928757 The Parsonage, Langley Burrell: 56
1740 Oxon	SU762825 63 & 65 Friday Street, Henley-on-Thames: 22, 28, 56
1741 Glos	ST683834 Sunset Cottage, Iron Acton: 25, 52, 56
1743 Surrey	TQ110599 Ham Manor, Cobham: 9, 13*b*, 17, 19, 24, 25
1743 Westm	SD319998 Yew Tree Farm, Coniston: 3, 9, 13*b*, 14, 17, 22, 25, 26, 28, 29, 45, 50*a*, 52
1744 Surrey	TQ045671 Old Parsonage, Chertsey: 11, 13*b*
1744 Sussex	TQ843236 Church House, Beckley: 3, 4, 9, 13*a*
1745 Mon	ST274970 Glyn-bran, Llanfecha Upper: 50*a*
1745 Suff	TM117591 House, The Street, Earl Stonham: 17, 24, 26,

	28, 34, 39, 52, 53, 56
1745 Surrey	SU997618 Brooklands House, Chobham: 3, 11, 17, 25, 52
1746 Middx	TQ033714 17 The Hythe, Staines: 24
1748 Yorks	NZ771049 Red House, Glaisdale: 3
1752 Durham	NY974235 High Green, Mickleton: 3, 6, 7, 8, 9, 13*b*, 18, 25, 39, 45, 49, 51, 52, 57
1754/5 Devon	SS666451 East Bodley Farm, Parracombe (cf 1739): 36*l*, 52
1756 Lancs	SD831392 Nabs House, Roughlee Booth: 13*b*
1756 Yorks	SE422423 Bramham Biggin, Bramham: 3, 9, 11, 12
1757 Surrey	SU944593 Bullhousen Farm, Bisley: 5, 6, 17, 19, 52, 56
1758 Sussex	TQ688301 18–20 Church Street, Ticehurst: 52
1760 Flints	SJ092700 Hafod-Tan-Eglwys, Bodfari: 25, 52
1763 Sussex	TQ853129 Hole Farm, Fairlight: 36*l*, 56